OUR COMMON COUNTRY

T0307649

OUR COMMON COUNTRY

MUTUAL GOOD WILL
IN AMERICA

BY

Warren G. Harding

EDITED BY
Warren G. Harding III

WITH AN INTRODUCTION BY
Robert H. Ferrell

UNIVERSITY OF MISSOURI PRESS

COLUMBIA AND LONDON

The Curators of the University of Missouri
University of Missouri Press, Columbia, Missouri 65201
Originally published in 1921 by Bobbs-Merrill Company
Printed and bound in the United States of America

5 4 3 2 1   07 06 05 04 03

Library of Congress Cataloging-in-Publication Data

Harding, Warren G. (Warren Gamaliel), 1865–1923.
    Our common country : mutual good will in America / by
Warren G. Harding ; edited by Warren G. Harding III; with an
Introduction by Robert H. Ferrell.
        p. cm.
Originally published: New York : Bobbs-Merrill Co., 1921.
Includes index.
        ISBN 0-8262-1454-1 (alk. paper)
    1. United States—Civilization—1918–1945.   2. National
characteristics, American.   3. United States—Social conditions—
1918–1932.   4. United States—Politics and government—1921–
1923.   I. Harding, Warren G., III.   II. Title.
    E169 .H26 2003
    973.91′4′092—dc21

                                                          2002015448

    ∞ This paper meets the requirements of the
American National Standard for Permanence of Paper
    for Printed Library Materials, z39.48, 1984.

DESIGNER: KRISTIE LEE
TYPESETTER: THE COMPOSING ROOM OF MICHIGAN, INC.
PRINTER AND BINDER: THE MAPLE-VAIL BOOK MANUFACTURING GROUP
TYPEFACE: ADOBE CASLON

Contents

PREFACE
by Warren G. Harding III   vii

INTRODUCTION
by Robert H. Ferrell   1

FOREWORD TO THE 1921 EDITION
by Frederick E. Schortemeier   7

I. RECONSECRATION TO GOD   13

II. BUSINESS AND GOVERNMENT   15

III. THE INSPIRATION OF LABOR   22

IV. AMERICAN AGRICULTURE   34

V. WHAT OF OUR CHILDREN   54

VI. THE PRESS AND THE PUBLIC   57

VII. THE THEATER   63

VIII. AMERICAN EDUCATION   69

IX. THE IMMIGRANT   73

X. CONSERVATION AND DEVELOPMENT   80

XI. SOCIAL JUSTICE   90

XII. THE VALUE OF PLAY   102

XIII. FRATERNITY   106

XIV. THE VILLAGE   112

XV. TWO WARS   115

XVI. THE MEANING OF THE ARMISTICE   117

XVII. THE FEDERAL CONSTITUTION   120

XVIII. THE NATIONAL CONSCIENCE   131

Index 135

PREFACE

Warren G. Harding III

In the autumn of 1920, with the United States challenged by postwar disunity and economic depression, Warren G. Harding—a man of strong personal, business, and political values and a remarkable ability to achieve—campaigned for the presidency. His platform promised a return to peace, prosperity, and opportunity. He inspired Americans with his call for America First and reassured them by advocating a return to prewar normalcy. Elected the twenty-ninth president, he began to work to bring his vision to reality, seeking to make the United States a prosperous nation in which all citizens would enjoy the benefits of equal opportunity.

Like his fellow Republican Abraham Lincoln before him, Harding believed he was charged with preserving the nation. In 1920 the dividing force was not secession but the yielding of governmental responsibilities as mandated under the proposed covenant of the League of Nations. He argued against making a commitment to the league unless appropriate reservations were enacted. It was his viewpoint that the destiny of the United States is to lead the world by example, not to force its ideas on others.

The success of Harding's America First program can be evaluated in terms of a simile used by the historian Henry Adams. A grandson and great-grandson of presidents, Adams proposed likening the American president to the captain of a ship at sea with a helm to grasp, a port to seek, and a course to steer. Harding's port, or vision, was to bring peace, prosperity, and opportunity to every American. His means to that end, or course to steer, encompassed both domestic and foreign policy. At home this meant reduction of the national debt, a balanced budget, efficiency in government through the newly created Bureau of the Budget, and lower taxes. The nation's international standing was improved by concluding peace treaties with Germany, Austria, and Turkey, formally ending the World War; supporting entry into the World Court; and negotiating the treaties of the Washington Conference of 1921–1922, which for the first time limited the strategic armaments of the world powers by restricting the tonnage and armaments of battleships. Proposed at the time of the presidential election of 1920, these goals were refined and realized during the two-and-one-half-year term that ended with Harding's untimely death in 1923.

We have learned of President Harding's life, ideas, and accomplishments from historians, politicians, and others who, inspired by one purpose or another, have examined his administration. Here, in *Our Common Country*, written by the president-elect himself in late 1920 between his election and his inauguration, we have an opportunity to gain knowledge and understanding of what he himself meant by "mutual good will and fortune in America."

Today there is a striking resemblance to this earlier time when the American nation was forced to evaluate itself and its role in the world. Surely in President Harding's words we can again find inspiration to steer the ship of state through perilous waters.

This edition follows the text of the original edition of 1921. All spellings and usage have been retained as President Harding presented his work; only obvious typographical errors have been corrected.

OUR COMMON COUNTRY

INTRODUCTION

Robert H. Ferrell

It is not often that a future president of the United States un-
dertakes a series of informal addresses—they were presented ex-
tempore—that catch the mood of the nation and say something
thoughtful about it. Such was the case with the addresses in
this book. Apart from their reference to 1920–1921, the period
during which the then senator from Ohio offered them, they
have a remarkable relevance to the country at the present time.

The years just after America's participation in World War I
are receding into the distant past, into the darker corridors of
the century that has just closed, and few people living today are
old enough to recall the nation's mood of that time. The veterans of that war have nearly passed off the scene, as years ago
happened to the Civil War veterans. I can remember, as a child
in the 1930s, seeing one of the last of the Civil War veterans—
an old (I then thought) man in a smashed-down hat sitting in
the back of an open automobile, looking out with sightless eyes.
The same is now true of the veterans of the war to which Senator Harding refers. Survivors might now number a few hundred, and all are at least centenarians.

The war was such a dominating presence at the time, and so

confusing too, because it did not turn out the way people thought it would. When America entered the war in 1917 there were flags everywhere—Fifth Avenue in New York was a riot of red, white, and blue with all of the shop windows decorated in patriotic themes. Across the continent, from the Atlantic to the Pacific, cities, towns, and villages rose to the occasion. It was, admittedly, a sudden change of outlook. During the time of American neutrality President Woodrow Wilson had told the country that war would not accomplish anything that was permanent, that Americans should be too proud to fight, and he was reelected in 1916 on slogans of "He kept us out of war" and "War in the east, peace in the west, thank God for Wilson." Then in a few weeks he began to speak of the country's rights on the seas, violated by the submarines of Imperial Germany that sank ships entering into German-defined zones around the British Isles and the Continent, this despite a virtual German promise to the president not to do such a thing. After the country went to war the president called for "force, force to the utmost, force without stint or limit, the righteous and triumphant force which shall make right the law of the world, and cast every selfish dominion down in the dust." Two million American soldiers went to France and fifty thousand died. The battle of the Meuse-Argonne, forty-seven days in the war's final phase, was the most costly battle in all of American history. It soon was followed by declarations from America's allies that the United States had not helped a great deal, that its contribution to the war was insignificant, compared to their own.

At this juncture the president's leadership collapsed. He had not been tactful with members of Congress, not given them a feeling that they, along with him, were leading the country. Indeed, he acted as if they were students in one of his classes at Princeton, where he had taught for twenty years before rising to the presidency. When he went to Paris and arranged the Treaty of Versailles, the peace treaty with Germany, and treaties with the other Central Powers, which included in their first twenty-six articles the constitution, known as the covenant, of a new world organization, the League of Nations, the Senate of the United States refused its consent. One of his adversaries, Senator William E. Borah of Idaho, said that the league should be twenty thousand leagues under the sea.

Nor were international affairs the only source of confusion to people of Harding's time. During the war the domestic economy had thrived. Immediately afterward it continued to rise, but boom was followed by bust. The index of wholesale commodity prices fell from 227.9 in 1920 to 150.6 in 1921, with 4.7 million Americans out of work. The national debt expanded from $1 billion to $26 billion, and for individuals of that era—unaccustomed to the philosophy that a national debt can be an unadulterated blessing by permitting the federal government to balance the debt against expenditures and an expected modest annual inflation—the country seemed to be going, to use a contemporary expression, to hell in a handbasket.

The historian Henry Adams, who died in 1917, had written that the twentieth century would see the pace of events increasing exponentially. He was unsure this was a good thing (actually he was unsure that life was a good thing). Adams's idea about the increasing torrent of events was correct—what a change from the eras of President John Adams and his son John Quincy Adams. As for the pessimism of the historian member of the family, by Harding's time the country agreed with him.

World War I indeed was a turning point in history. A historian of our own time, John Lukacs, has written that it was the great turning point, that we are seeing now the end of an age that began with the Renaissance and Reformation in which individuals were central to history, rather than nations. The war of 1914–1918 witnessed the triumph not of communism, a trivial event in history, but of nationalism, soon of a virulent sort in Nazi Germany. The triumph of nationalism lifted the floodgates of evil that had been contained ever since medieval times.

Harding spoke to his own time and yet, as we now can see, he spoke to our own. The confusions of the present are much like those of 1920–1921.

Warren Harding was a remarkable president, beloved in his time, maligned in the years after his death. He was born in the last year of the Civil War, near the village of Blooming Grove, in Ohio. He grew up in another Ohio hamlet, Caledonia, attended an academy, Ohio Central College in Iberia, and removed to a town turning into a city, Marion, where he purchased a failing weekly newspaper, the *Star*. With the assistance of his wife, the former Florence Kling, he changed it into a prosperous daily; Florence was the manager and her husband gathered the news. A public speaker of striking ability, who made every member of an audience think that he was speaking directly to that person, he took an interest in politics and served two terms in the Ohio senate and another as lieutenant governor. For a decade thereafter he pursued his newspaper work. In 1914 he ran for election to the U.S. Senate, the first time such was possible after a constitutional amendment did away with election by the state legislature. He won by a tremendous majority, one hundred thousand votes. In 1920 when two strong candidates for the presidency battled each other to a standstill at the Republican convention in Chicago, his time came and he was nominated. He was elected by the largest popular majority in the history of the presidency until the triumph of President Franklin D. Roosevelt over Governor Alf Landon of Kansas in 1936.

Harding was an immensely popular president. He followed the precepts of his speeches of 1920–1921, symbolized by the word *normalcy* (which he did not invent). His administration brought a formal end to the World War, so far as concerned the United States, by the Treaty of Berlin with Germany and similar treaties with the other former Central Powers. He sponsored the Washington Naval Conference of 1921–1922, the first occasion when a conference limited the size and guns of fighting ships, in this instance battleships and a novel ship known as the aircraft carrier. The Harding administration instituted the Bureau of the Budget, bringing order to the departmental and bureau requests that had disgraced budget making for decades.

Harding was the first American president to visit Alaska, and he died in San Francisco on his return journey. He had not understood how ill he had been while in the presidency. When he took office in 1921 his systolic blood pressure had risen to 180, and by early 1923 he could not sleep without being propped up with pillows. He evidently suffered a heart attack en route to San Francisco by train after the Alaska tour. Ill upon arrival, he insisted on walking from the presidential Pullman to a waiting automobile and at the Palace Hotel walked up the steps, through the lobby to the elevator, thence to his rooms, where he collapsed and in a few days died, of a massive heart attack.

It was after this hardworking, intelligent, one might well say inspired—as the addresses illustrate—president died that the slanderers, for their several reasons, assaulted his reputation. In that sense Harding died twice, for there was his physical death and then the death of his reputation. He was accused of arranging the sale of naval oil reserves to private oilmen, an act with which he had almost nothing to do. A minor scandal in the Veterans' Bureau—what presidential administration has not had a scandal or two?—was credited to him, although he had ousted the administrator of the bureau. He was accused of collaboration with his attorney general, Harry M. Daugherty, in a fund maintained in a bank owned by Daugherty's brother in Washington Court House, Ohio, near Columbus; Daugherty had been Harding's campaign manager in 1920, almost certainly suffered a stroke in early 1923, and was incapable of defending himself. Meanwhile other scandalmongers were at work. In 1927 a young woman who had known Harding in Marion accused him, in a book of doubtful veracity and most lucrative to the author, of fathering her child. In 1930 a convicted felon, convicted again for extortion in the Lindbergh kidnapping case of 1934, and who died in prison, published a book that he did not write and his ghost disowned, in which he asserted that Harding had been poisoned by his wife in San Francisco (where, for the record, let it be said that five physicians were in attendance).

Sadly, concerning the reputation of President Harding, the author of these luminous addresses, it is necessary to add that the canards, public and private, have been repeated by newspaper reporters, writers, historians, and political scientists down to the present day.

But to return to the addresses that together constitute *Our Common Country*. They are carefully thought out and straightforward. There is nothing emotional about them, or occasional; they are what the country needed in Harding's time, and what it needs now.

FOREWORD TO THE 1921 EDITION

Frederick E. Schortemeier

Under the leadership of President Harding, America is at the threshold of an era of good will. Several of our presidents have performed greater services for America than befell their lot as its chief executive in an administrative capacity by leading in the development of the moral forces of our country. Harding's greatest service to his country at home will come in the awakening of the American conscience toward the mutual good will of Americans, one for the other. He would end the day of jealous rivalries, of class detriment, of group supremacy, of greed, and lead the way in making popular throughout America understanding, cooperation and good will toward men.

Warren Harding has already become known to the American people as a strong nationalist in international relations. It is the purpose in this volume to give to the American people in the president's own words his conception of the proper course for the people of America in their domestic relations. Just as Harding has taken the leadership in the preservation of the nationality of the United States, so he will come to be known as the foremost advocate of a national appeal toward a common understanding, a mutuality of interests on the part of all the Amer-

ican people, the end of class consciousness, and the prosperity
and happiness of all Americans, everywhere.

Those Americans who seek the day of a more widely applied
good will in America, who fervently hope for the time when no
group of our people will place its own interests above the common weal of all the people where the interests conflict, will find
in Harding their staunchest advocate. This fundamental conception of the proper American relationship is shown in everything Harding thinks and says and does. Harding hopes for the
utter abolition of class. He seeks to encourage the fullest cooperation by preaching the gospel of understanding. His great purpose is to construe and develop the desire for a common good
fortune in America. "I wish it distinctly noted," said the president, shortly after his nomination, "that I shall say nothing to
one group of fellow citizens which I could not as cordially utter
to another. So far as I can be helpful it shall be along the line of
promoting the good fortunes of all the American people. We
can not prosper one group and imperil another. We can not
have, we must not have, a menacing class consciousness in
America. I like to think of an America where every citizen's
pride in power and resources, in influence and progress, is
founded in what can be done for our people, all the people.
Good Government means the welfare of all of its citizens."

Harding seeks in America the application of those simple
virtues in our national life which are essentially necessary to the
life of a successful individual. He is sounding the call for the application of the common weal. He looks forward to the day
when no class of our people will seek to advance its own interests to the detriment of all the people. He wants a contented,
prosperous, happy America in which every individual and every
group of individuals will desire in good conscience to aid and
prosper the lot of all other Americans.

This volume seeks to present to the American public the

views of their president upon numerous phases of American life, and would show that in addition to entertaining definite ideas for the advancement of the welfare of our varied groups of citizens, Harding hopes to point the way toward the mutual good fortune of all Americans. He would prosper the farmer, the business man, the laborer, as such, to the fullest possible extent, but only so far as is consistent with the welfare of all other Americans. He is ready to lead in that most vital and timely American undertaking which has for its purpose the end of classism and the development of all that is good for all Americans, under all circumstances, in all walks of life and in every conceivable situation.

Harding proclaims anew the equality of opportunity. From his own life's experiences, he knows whereof he speaks. He acclaims individual and personal honesty as the greatest of all American assets. He hopes for an American reconsecration to faith in God. He longs for the day when every American genuinely and sincerely wishes well for every other American citizen. He aspires to develop in America a contented, happy people, who find their delight in their belief in and devotion to good will for all Americans. To him every American life is sacred and is entitled to the fullest opportunity for development. "If a wise God notes a sparrow's fall, no life can be so obscure and humble that it shall become of no consequence to America," is Harding's conception. He seeks the best and the most for every human who has been fortunate enough to come beneath the folds of the American flag.

Besides his consuming desire for the common weal in America, Harding has very definite ideas for its development. He wants a common understanding between employer and employee. He desires the promotion of those measures which make better the lot of American women and children, which feed and clothe our unfortunates and which buoy their spirits. He encourages play and urges honest work. He delights in the enthusiasms of accomplishment. He would have a normal America in which those rigid American virtues of honesty, understanding, cooperation and good will are popular among Americans.

As president of the United States he would lead to "where every one plays his part with soul and enthusiasm, no matter how insignificant that part may be, so that out of the grouped endeavor comes the perfect offering." Harding is ready to lead the moral forces of America in the further development of our common country, in the establishment of mutual good will in America.

Our Common Country

RECONSECRATION TO GOD

A Message and a Dedication

I do not believe there is any other influence so much needed in a tumultuous world as a reconsecration to God Almighty. I rejoice that America is free in religion. We boast our civil liberty and our political independence, but when we contemplate world conditions to-day the best thing in this Republic is religious freedom.

Sometimes I think the world has gone adrift from its moorings religiously, and I know it will help if we have a revival of religious faith. I want a government that is just, and I don't think a government can be just if it does not have somehow a contact with Omnipotent God.

I know how some of you of the church have been quite carried away by the proposal of a new world relationship. You never stopped to think that in the conception of Versailles there was no recognition of God Almighty. Just as we of America have builded by recognizing Him, the best relationship of the world must be builded upon recognition of the same God.

I have every faith that our nation will take its fitting place in an association of nations for world peace, and I believe that we are going to be able to do it without the surrender of anything we hold dear as a heritage of the American people.

I don't like to talk about religion, just for the sake of conversation, but I do believe that we need more of it in our American life, more of it in government,—the real spirit of it. I think there should be more of the "Do unto others as you would be done by" spirit of service.

It might interest you to know that, while I have always been a great reader of the Bible, I have never read it so closely as in the last weeks, when my mind has been bent upon the work I must shortly take up. I have obtained a good deal of inspiration from the Psalms of David and from many passages of the four gospels, and there's still wisdom in the sayings of old Solomon.

I don't intend to come as the finest exemplar of what we ought to be, but I rejoice in the inheritance of a religious belief and I don't mind saying that I gladly go to God Almighty for guidance and strength in the responsibilities that are coming to me.

BUSINESS AND GOVERNMENT
A Message for Business Men

We are the great business nation of the world. We shall be able to save that business and prosper it by a fair measure of common sense, and we ought and must do it. We will preserve a willingness to listen to the will of the people, and will construe the desire for a common good fortune to mean the necessary good fortune of business, which is the life-blood of material existence.

American business is not big business. Wilful folly has been in those persons in distended power over our national affairs who have spoken of American business as if it were a large and selfish interest seeking special privileges, and who, on that basis, have put their bungling hands upon its throat and tried tinkering and experimenting with it, and abusing it and treating it with suspicion. Let us put an end to holding success to be a crime.

It will be the American people who will do this because American business is everybody's business. Nearly nine-tenths of those who depend for their living and the legitimate fruits of their labors in American manufacturing are the wage-earners. The blow directed at American business, the pulling and hauling of American business by weird economic and social theories, is less menacing, for instance, to the one-tenth who in manufacturing are business executives than it is to the nine-tenths who are our American laborers.

The big business of America is the little business of America. The last available census figures show that more than sixty per cent of our factories were little plants, none of which turned out more than $100,000 of products. Only twenty-five per cent of our plants were even doing business as corporations. The average number of workers employed was twenty-five. When we come to analyze what we mean by American business we find out that we mean the daily work of the nation, most of it undertaken in the factory and on the farm in small units. We find out that we even mean the business of the home and of the housewife, and that American business is everybody's business. It is more than that. It is the work of every worker, clothes for his back, food for his mouth.

We must face the new task. We have had a fever of high prices and excessive production out of the sacrificed billions of treasures and millions of lives, but the reconstruction must be sober business, founded on unchanging principle. We must summon the best abilities of America to put America back on the main road, and to remove the debris of the last eight years, and to keep our industries running, and to restore the proper ratio of prosperity to our American agriculture so that it can again bid for good American standard labor.

If our memory is directed again to 1914, we will recall that world war alone saved us from a disaster in peace. We were sharpening our wits in competition with the world, as the President then expressed it, but we dulled our capacity to buy, then war saved us psychologically and commercially; but to-day we are at peace, actual though not proclaimed, and our problems are the problems of peace.

We must always exact, from ourselves and our business, high, honorable and fair dealing by law, and by law's rigid enforcement when necessary, but we must repeal and wipe out a mass of executive orders and laws which, failing to serve effectively that purpose, serve only to leave American business in anxiety, uncertainty and darkness.

We must readjust our tariff, and this time with especial regard for the new economic menace to our American agriculture as well as manufacturing.

We must readjust our internal taxation, especially the excess profits tax, to remove the burdens it imposes upon the will to create and produce, whether that will is the will of the big corporation, of the small corporation, or of the individual.

We must uproot from our national government the yearning to undertake enterprises and experiments which were never intended as the work of our government, which have proved ineffective to a point which sickens us all, and which our government is incapable of performing without wreckage or chaos. Of necessity the machinery of government expands as we grow in numbers as a people, but before government expands in bureaucratic control of business its sponsors ought first to demonstrate a capacity to conduct the business of the government. When government itself has a budget of more than three billions a year, in times of peace, it has a business of its own to look after—and it needs looking after—without seeking new fields to conquer until it has proved capacity for the tasks it must perform.

We must, instead of such experiments, establish a closer understanding between American government and American business, so that one may serve the other, and the other obey and seek cooperation.

We must give government cooperation to business, we must protect American business at home, and we must aid and protect it abroad by the upbuilding of our merchant marine, and a restoration of our self-respecting measure of American protection to her citizens wherever they may go upon righteous errands.

We must build our economic life into new strength and we must do it so that our prosperity shall not be the prosperity of profiteers nor of special privilege.

We must do it so that abroad we are known not as a nation strutting under a plumage of fine words, but as one that knits friendly and peaceful relations by the shuttle of honorable deeds.

We must do it so that at home our economic life yields opportunity to every man not to have that which he has not earned, whether he be the capitalist or the humblest laborer, but to have a share in prosperity based upon his own merit, capacity and worth—under the eternal spirit of "America First."

American business has suffered from staggering blows because of too much ineffective meddling by government, and it is equally true that good government has almost been allowed to die on our hands, because it has not utilized the first sound principles of American business.

The government of the United States, of this nation of ours, which should be an example of American good sense and sound organization, has been allowed to degenerate into an inadequate piece of administrative machinery. While we have heard preaching to all the nations of the earth, which, to put it mildly, has been adequate indeed, the back of our leadership has been turned on the bad example we have set before the world in the conduct of our own affairs. I refer only to the deplorable impairment which has been given our time-tested democratic institutions by robbing our representative government of its place in our republic in order to fatten administrative authority and replace the will of the people by the will of the wilful.

The government has engaged in prodigal waste. The American people pay. It has kept its overstuffed bureaus and departments, many of which are doing overlapping work, in a prime condition of reckless inefficiency. The American people pay. It has engaged in all kinds of costly bungling experiments of government management and ownership of enterprises which other management could do better. The American people pay. It has allowed worthy federal employees, particularly those who are skilled, such as chemists and agricultural experts, to go so badly paid by the government that they have left the service. The American people have to bear the cost. It has poured forth our national treasure into the yawning emptiness of unpreparedness for war and unpreparedness for peace. It has spent our money and failed to do business, while the prodigal flow went on. The American people have paid, and are paying. With a return to sanity we now have another task before us in making the administrative part of our government one in which a people, proud of its abilities in business, can take pride.

We must not let our administrative government crack under the load of its new burdens or those that our future may place upon it. It has been cracking badly. To repair it is the business of every American—not only because of pride, but also because he pays for it, and is entitled to good government without waste.

We have declared for a system of planning our expenditures so that overlapping and leakage and inefficiency shall be revealed before they occur. This national budget plan we must put into force.

We must put our postal service upon a new basis, and extend the merit system in the choice and promotion of federal employees.

We must not only lop off useless jobs, but we must so reward efficiency and value among our public service employees that we may continue to have their loyalty because we have given decent pay and the expectation of promotion when promotion is earned.

We must conduct a careful scrutiny of our great executive departments to plan so that similar labors shall not be duplicated and so that similar functions shall be grouped and not scattered.

We must go to men who know, for advice in administrative improvement; we must have to aid us more men trained in agriculture, more technical men, more men who know business and the practises of commerce and trade.

I look upon the responsibility of an executive as being based first of all upon his ability, together with that of capable men called to execute. An executive officer of any other than government business would be discharged if he allowed paralysis and perversion of the functioning of that business, while he and his followers were engaged in addressing advice to the neighbors.

Let them who say that the American people are not awake to these matters take new counsel. The government is the people's business, and they will not see it broken down. The government is the concern of every American—of every man, woman and child. We are shareholders in it and we are looking forward with relief to an end of mismanagement.

This great federal machine has grown up in a century of haphazard expansion, until, as recently described, it resembles "an antiquated central building with a large number of surrounding sheds and cottages, overcrowded with overlapping officials and saturated with methods of organization and administration fully fifty years behind the times."

An eminent senator once said he could substitute his private business methods for government practises and save hundreds of millions. It was thought to be true when he said it, and we might treble the figures for the saving now.

Here in America we have developed the most proficient and

most efficient types of business organization and administration in the world; they have shown the greatest capacity for administrative vision. We mean to call that administrative quality and fitness into the service of the government, and establish an advance in government business, not merely talk about government progress.

Conditions are calling, capabilities await, the needs are urging and we pledge a new order—a business government, with business efficiency, and a business concern for public approval.

THE INSPIRATION OF LABOR
A Message for Those Who Toil

Life is labor, or labor is life, whichever is preferred. Men speak of the labor issue as paramount or imperious or critical—it is always the big thing because it is the process of all progress and attainment, and has been since the world began. The advocate of excessively-reduced periods of labor simply proposes to slow down human attainment, because labor is the agency of all attainment. If by some miracle of agreement we could reduce the hours of labor to four per day—I speak of labor now in the sense of that which is employed for pay—the live, progressive, civilization-creating, progressive labor would have to go on working twice or thrice that time, because labor is the ferment of human development. No one will challenge these general truths, but we do have a conflict of opinion as to how labor shall be employed and the measure of its compensation.

I wish it distinctly noted that I shall say nothing to one group of fellow citizens which I could not as cordially utter to another. It was my good fortune to have a call from a committee representing several American farm organizations, and I told them frankly I preferred to greet them as fellow-Americans rather than farmers, because our big thought must be of American consumers, they among them. They were concerned in producing food, which is of first concern to all America. I am thinking of industrial America, that industrial America in which every one of our hundred millions is deeply concerned, and the good fortune of whose workers is of highest interest to our people as a whole.

Do not let anyone ever tell you that any political party is insensible to the cause of labor. Parties are the agencies of government, and men who assume public responsibility are deeply anxious about the common weal. Demagogues or agitators, most of whom are agitating for the profit therein, "Reds" or reactionaries, all of them deny the high intent and genuine concern of parties and government for the highest good fortunes of all the people. Frankly, I do not think any party is indifferent or unmindful. The only difference is in the program for the greatest good. I want you to understand me definitely. So far as I can be helpful it shall be along the line of promoting the good fortunes of all the American people, because in common good fortune, made secure, we have the field in which to work to adjust the distribution of rewards to the highest conception of fairness and justice.

Let me repeat a public utterance of mine. Noting the advanced ground reached through the sufferings and sacrifices of the World War, I said we contemplated a new level, a new order, and would never return to the old pre-war conditions. No such return has ever been recorded in all history. I spoke of high wages, and said I wished the existing high scale to remain, on one explicit condition—that for the high wage, the American workman shall give to his task the highest degree of efficiency. There isn't any other solution. There isn't any other way to keep wages high and lower the cost of living to any appreciable degree.

The menace of the present day is inefficient production. I am not advocating the driving, slavish period of toil, which saps men's energies and oppresses the spirit, but I do advocate honest, efficient return for proper pay. I hold that the slacker, the loafer on the job, is not only the greatest obstacle to labor's advancement, but he is cheating his fellows more than he does his employer. The workman who deliberately adds to costs robs a fellow workman who must buy, and impedes the way to that ideal condition where wage exceeds the cost of living, and there is a balance for the bank account, for home acquirement and indulgence in amusement, diversion and the becoming luxuries which contribute to the ideal life.

Let no one beguile you with dreams of idleness, of the passing of employment or the abolition of employer and employee. Life without toil, if possible, would be an intolerable existence. Work is the supreme engagement, the sublime luxury of life. And there will be employers so long as there is leadership among men, and there will be employees until human progress is paralyzed and the development of human kind dies on one common altar of mediocrity. Our problem then is to find the high order of employment, the ideal relationship, the conditions under which we may work to the highest attainment and the greatest common good for all concerned.

It is utterly false to assume that labor and capital are in deadly conflict. Such a preachment comes from those who would destroy our social system. More, these two elements do not constitute alone the fabric of our industrial life, and neither of them, alone, ever added to the treasure of mankind. The element of management is as essential to present-day industrial success, amid modern complexities, as breath to the human body. And indissolubly linked with these three is the consuming public.

It is not important to establish which element comes first, since each is essential to the other. We do know that labor, the human element, is of deepest public concern. Hence it is that

American public opinion, which is invariably the ruling force in popular government, when deliberately crystallized, wishes the labor forces to be satisfied. Not contented, because contentment is the awaiting avenue to paralysis, but so satisfied that there is a soul of interest in all our employments.

The deplorable side of modern industry, with gigantic factory and the productive machinery, is that too many men are toiling like machines at work. There ought to be more in a day's work than the mere grind and the pay therefor, even though the pay is generous. Men ought to know a pride in the thing done. There ought to be inspiration to skill and glory in accomplishment. One ought to have before him the goal of being best in his line. The mere fulfillment of the requirements to hold a job never made superintendent or led to a captaincy in all the world of employment. Contentment with a job, with eyes riveted on pay day, without enthusiasm to accomplish or desire to excel, never made an advance for any man anywhere.

The big inspiration in life is to get on. We can not get on all alike or be regarded precisely alike. God Almighty never intended it to be so, else He had made us all alike. But we may get on according to our talent, our capacity, and our industry, and out of the advancement of those who lead, must come higher standards for all.

I have no patience with those who commend the levels of mediocrity. That would halt the whole human procession. I can read the aspirations in many a breast. Search the hearts of the parenthood. Fathers and mothers are thinking of their children, and they want them to get on. They often deny themselves to educate their children and ultimately find compensation in that denial. They educate so that sons and daughters may do better than they—it is the natural desire of aspiring life. This is why the world advances. This is the soul of advancing civilization. When men tell you this is the privilege of the few, they challenge your intelligence. It is the opportunity of all. Not all avail themselves, but the opportunity beckons.

I have seen my home city grow from the village of four thousand to the city of thirty thousand. I know the men who are the captains of industry and the commanders of trade and the leaders of finance. I have associated with the head of one great concern when he was toiling for seventy-five cents a day as a youth in the shops. I have seen another at the bench, and still another trying to make the pay envelope meet his obligations. I knew one bank leader as the boy who swept out and did the chores, another as a dollarless farmer boy, another as a struggling youth no more favored than the poorest boy. What's the explanation? Industry, thrift, love of work, interest in tasks, ambition to get on.

I wish I could plant the gospel of loyalty to work and interest in accomplishment. It is the ambition to succeed, the determination to do the most and best—these speed men on to the heights. The pity is that we do not have enough of it under modern conditions. There is too much mechanical grind, too little contact between employer and employee, too little understanding of their mutuality of interest and their joint triumph in success. I hail with equal satisfaction the workman who has pride in the factory and its output, and the employer who has pride and sympathetic interest in his workmen. I want to stress the need of pride. There is little enough to inspire under our modern system, and I want to magnify all there is. And above all else I want American workmen to feel that American products are the best in the world. There is only a touch of satisfaction to say our output is biggest, but it sets the heart aglow to proclaim America's output is the best.

I am sorry the old, intimate contact between employer and employee is gone. When there was intimate touch there was little or rare misunderstanding. I wish we could have the intimacy restored, not in the old way, but through a joint committee of employers and employees, not to run the business, but to promote and maintain the mutuality of interest and the fullest understanding. Herein lies the surest remedy for the most of our ills. Nay, more, I will put it more strongly, I have spoken the *preventive*, the understanding which prevents disputes, or settles them on the spot.

I never had any trouble with our labor forces in the printing line, though our "boys and girls" have been organized for seventeen years. We know each other pretty well. And yet, with all our intimacy and our freedom from disputes, I may not understand them as I ought nor do they understand all they ought. Let me give an example, because it will illustrate the need of understanding. The basic material, the one thing we must have in the newspaper business, is print paper. There has been a shortage of production and the market has been wild. We contracted for our annual supply, but we could not add the amount necessary to meet our normal growth. To meet the volume of business and keep all our men employed we had to buy extra print paper as best we could, and the excess above the contract cost was sufficient to pay out three hundred dollars additional wage to every workman in the shop. But we were obliged to meet so excessive an outlay, and could not pass it on to readers, yet no workman had to bear any share of the strain. Never forget that there are two sides, and I want each to understand the other. I want employers to know what is in the hearts of the workman—their aspirations, their trails, their problems—all the things essential to concord and good spirit.

To be specific, the need of to-day is the extension by employers of the principle that each job in the big plant is a little business of its own. The reason men in modern, specialized industry go crazy from lack of self-expression is that they are allowed to be mere mechanical motion-makers. They ought to be taught by employers the significance of this job—its unit costs, its relations to other operations, the ways to its greater efficiency. In a word the employer owes it to his men to make them feel that each job stops being an enemy of the man and becomes his associate and friend, and the success achieved opens the way for his looked-for advancement.

The world is thinking about means to prevent war among nations, and we approve, and share the aspiration. But America is also thinking about preventing industrial conflict and all attending waste, suffering and anxiety. The matter has become of interest to the public, even more than the forces engaged in any conflict.

Our observation is, as an eminent labor leader has said, that "all strikes sooner or later are settled around a table; then why not get around a table before the strike begins?"

We can not have compulsory arbitration, because all parties must consent to establish arbitration and enforce its conclusions. I think we can have and ought to have, voluntary volitional arbitration. The best thought of the day commends this way to settlement.

In the broad sense labor's business is selling its skilled or unskilled endeavor, and the basic cost is the cost of living. What labor receives over and above cost of living is pay for its preparation, and a profit for its inspiration.

The insistent thought is to add to this profit, to widen the difference between mere cost and the wage received. All the influence and the organization in the world will not equalize a living cost among a hundred millions. Rentals, until home-owning becomes more wide-spread—as I hope it will become wide-spread—vary according to localities and conditions. The wage scale which contemplates a rental cost in one place might be wholly inadequate to meet the cost in another and a nationalized scale would work an injustice. This point was developed in the recent railway controversies, and proved some very real grievances which the people had not dreamed.

This brings me to the subject of railway legislation, and the enactment of the Cummins-Esch Bill restoring the railways to the lawful owners. We owed it to the railway owners to restore their property, seized for war service, just as we owe the return of the people's money invested in government loans. In free and thoughtful America we do not take advantage of war's tumult to change the regular order of things. I am well aware that many earnest railway workers and advocates of the Socialist plan preferred to take the railroads and put them under the operation of the employees, but that was not keeping faith with America or American promises. We were honor bound to make the return. I favored it for the additional reason that I do not believe in government ownership.

The government must do many things, but it has enough to do without invading the field of private activity, not, at any rate, until government demonstrates its capacity for efficiency.

I do not pretend to say the railway act is perfect; indeed, I know it is not. But Congress was dealing with a problem of first importance, and it had to speed the legislation. There was the conflict of many minds as it was right there should be, and the final act was a compromise. Nevertheless, I believe it to be a good law and cordially supported it. Many railway labor leaders have cried out against it, but I can only wonder why, except for the fundamental objection to the release of government operation.

Let us try out the act and the railway restoration in patience. If we have fallen short, the conscience of America will sanction every modification needed to aim at perfection. America wants her railway workmen justly treated, and will tolerate nothing less, and America wants her honest investments properly protected, with justice to every agency employed in this great machine of railway transportation.

I have said it before, and I repeat it now, I want the American railway workers to know the best possible working conditions and to be the best paid in the world. Our food, our activities, our exchanges, so much depend on the great railway operations, and above all else, all who travel trust their lives to railway skill and fidelity. Ours ought to be, and must be, the best in the world.

I believe in the protective policy which prospers America first, and exalts American standards of wage and American standards of living high above the Old World. We had little thought of these things during the war, because America was exporting instead of importing—shipping out instead of shipping in—but it will soon be a different situation in the world exchange. I do not object to humanity seeking equalized standards of employment and living, but I do insist on Old World standards being raised to ours, not ours lowered to the Old World.

Our enormous balance of trade with foreign nations is fast receding and peoples who seek recuperation from war's wastes and bankruptcy are expecting to sell to us to recuperate, because our people are the ablest to buy in all the world. One must admit the promise of a cheaper cost of living if Europe's cheaper-made merchandise is brought to our markets. But note the peril to labor! If we buy abroad, we will slacken production at home, and slackened production means diminished employment, and growing idleness and all attending disappointments. I want to cheapen the cost of living as much as any one in all the land, but I do not wish it cheapened by the processes of unemployment and lowered standards of American labor.

Pray, do not even believe you are injuring yourself by giving full return for your employment. The call is for maximum production, and factory success is your success. Do not scale down to the inefficient and incapable. Let us train up and build up to the heights of the efficient.

What is the big inspiration in life? The natural desire to excel. Why do we applaud Babe Ruth? Because he has batted out more home runs in a season than any ball player on earth. If you were going to play ball, you wouldn't try to bat at one hundred fifty to two hundred, you would rather be a Babe Ruth. But men say that's different from the humdrum of toil. Well, that's why I am arguing the end of humdrum toil by striving for the heights. The workman who performs his tasks better than another has satisfaction in his soul, and he will not long escape the notice that brings him advancement.

Many other things will help to reduce living cost. I want to see profiteering isolated and punished. It is a moral wrong and an economic robbery. The man who practises profiteering is false in business and to country. I do not know of a deadlier foe to our common country, because he creates the unrest that threatens from within and emphasizes the appeal to class.

Reduced cost of government will help, and we can reduce cost of government by quitting the play of politics with the nation's bread and butter. Stage assaults on profiteering, mostly dealing with petty offenders, do not deeply impress the country, and sugar agreements which add a billion to our sugar bills for a year do not indicate a know-how which entitles the bunglers to hold their jobs.

I have not come with promises. I can not pledge you the impossible, and do not mean to suggest the impractical. I can only preach the gospel of understanding practically applied. In public service, I have always been ready to hear the appeal of all Americans, and labor will find an ever-ready period to be heard, not for labor alone, but for the good of all our people. We can not prosper one group and imperil another. We can not have, we must not have, a menacing class consciousness. When we look each other in the face, soberly contemplating the great web of American life, we see that the good of one is the fortune of all.

Our system is all right; it is the judgment of the ages, and here in America we have wrought the supreme achievement. There are abuses, perhaps there ever will be. Greed develops and robbery breaks out amid all great processions. Our business is to strike at greed, and outlaw robbery, and correct the abuses, without destroying the temple in which we abide.

I do not think we can fabricate the perfect world, but we can and we mean to make it better from day to day and year to year. I do not blow you a bubble of imaginary equality of men or women, but I do proclaim equality of opportunity, proved in America in making America the best land of hope in all the world. The fair chance is here. It isn't in a particular craft, it isn't alone in the closed shop, it isn't in the offerings of the law, it isn't in the revolutionary proposals of those who threaten destruction in return for liberty's blessings. It is in honest endeavor, in thrift, in lofty aspiration, and a resolute determination to do, and to get on in the world.

I believe in unionism, I believe in collective bargaining. I believe the two have combined to speed labor toward its just rewards. But I do not believe in labor's domination of business or government any more than I believe that capital should dominate. We had our time at that, and we learned the danger and ended it. We do not want to substitute one class for another, we want to put an end to classes.

We live in an era of collective endeavor. Capital led the way, and labor's organization was not only natural, but necessary. It has done more than serve its membership, it has riveted the thoughtful attention of America to social justice and brought the fruits thereof.

I hold that the advancement of labor's cause in America challenges all the world. We have made, of course, a few thousand millionaires, but we made millions of self-reliant, advancing, creative Americans. The luxury of yesterday is the accepted necessity of to-day. I struggled to own a motor-car after I had been an employer for twenty years, and workmen nowadays drive to their tasks at thirty, without realizing the transformation. The progress is the miracle of American opportunity. I want to hold to fundamentals, strike at any developing inequality and halt assault on our system, then go on to greater things.

The way is open. Opportunity is calling, and harmonized capital and labor and management will clear the waiting paths, and individual resolution, the heritage of American freedom, will speed us on. If we only hold fast to the fundamentals, the pride of to-day may be a greater glory to-morrow, and ultimately we shall approach that combination of achievement and happiness for all men which is the divine plan for the triumphs of earth and life and human endeavor.

AMERICAN AGRICULTURE
A Message for Farmers

I address you not as farmers but as patriotic citizens of the United States. Every word that I say to you is addressed not to your welfare alone, but to the welfare of every man, woman and child, and to the welfare of the future citizens of our country.

I deplore the use in political campaigns or in public administration of special appeals and of special interests. I deplore any foreign policy which tends to group together those of foreign blood according to their nativity. I deplore undue meddling in the affairs of other nations, which may, some day in a future election, result in a hyphenated vote controlling the balance of power which may be delivered to that candidate who is most supine in the face of un-American pressure. I deplore class appeals at home. I deplore the soviet idea, and the compromises and encouragements which we have seen extended to it.

When the responsibility for leadership in putting America back on to the main road, was placed upon me, I said to myself that we must all unite under the slogan "America First." When I say America First I mean not only that America maintain her own independence and be first in fulfilling her obligations to the world, by deeds rather than words, and by example rather than preaching, but I mean that at home any special interest, any class, any group of our citizenship that has arrayed itself against the interests of all, must learn that at home, as well as abroad, America First has a meaning, profound, and, with God's aid, everlasting.

It is true that you, the farmers of this country, and I are charged with an obligation of program and definite action that fosters the welfare of all America, the welfare of the man who lives in the house with the red barn and the productive fields behind it, and also the welfare of the man who in a crowded industrial city, comes home at nightfall to climb the stairs to his fourth-floor home, behind the fire escapes, with hunger in the body.

I desire with all my heart to speak for the consumer when I speak of American agriculture. I desire to put aside platitudes, all the poetic tradition about the worth and merits of the honest farmer. Honesty is not peculiar to any occupation. I desire to awake the country to the menaces to its future unless American agriculture is preserved, and above nonsense and false promises and prodigal waste and dictatorial powers, all of which have smothered the farmer, as they have smothered us all, and overworked executive powers. I desire, in this great agricultural problem as in all our national problems, to go back to the functions of our Republic and of our representative system. I want to restore the will of the people. And under the restoration, I desire to deal with all our great problems, not in the twilight of generalities, but in the full sunlight of definition and forward marching.

With the agriculture of the United States—the basic industry—I am deeply concerned. If history does not deceive us by changing repetitions of her precepts, a nation lives no longer than her agricultural health abides. It is the soil that is our mother, and the mother of nations; it is land hunger that founds revolutions, anarchy and decay. We must look our land problems and farming situation squarely in the face and act bravely and wisely and promptly. In doing so, you and I must turn to the consumers of the United States and say, "This is your problem and your posterity's problem as well as ours."

The day of land hunger has come. The day when we see before us the spectacle of the land-owing farmer being displaced by capitalistic speculation in land and the soil-exhausting and landlord-exploited tenant farmer has come. The day when the share of the American farmer in whatever is left of prosperity has been overtopped by the share taken by our industrial production, has come. The day when industry outbids agriculture for labor has come. The day when the profit of the farmer has been cut down and the price to the consumer has been lifted up, has come. The day when bad and wasteful distribution between producer and consumer, and the day of too much unrighteous profiteering, by too many unnecessary middlemen, has come. The day when production of our soil must be protected against the soil products of countries of low standards of living, has come.

These conditions call for wise action on the part of government. They call for good counsel. They call for the presence of the American farmer in our government offices, administrative and representative. They call for extension of the farm loan principle, not only in the case of the man who already owns a farm, but to worthy Americans who want to acquire farms. In other words, they call for capital available to the farmers of America as a bulwark against the exploits of capital available to the land speculator.

Furthermore, these conditions call for a willingness of all Americans to act together in restoring to American agriculture a prosperity that will keep the land owner and land worker upon our soil. We must obliterate the picture of the year 1920, when we have allowed the labor of the farm-wife and young girls and old women to be the substitute for normal farm labor. The women have helped to guarantee to consumers of the United States and dependent nations their full food supply, and though it is a monument to them we must find ways to restore a more normal and a more American labor supply to our farms.

I believe that the American people, through their government and otherwise, not only in behalf of the farmer but in behalf of their own welfare, and the pocketbooks of the consumers of America, will encourage, make lawful, and stimulate cooperative buying, cooperative distribution, and cooperative selling of farm products.

Industry has been organized; labor has been organized; cooperation within industry and within labor, and indeed, cooperation between the two, is far advanced. I do not contemplate the organization of the farmers and consumers of this country as a step toward organization of special interests to obtain special favors. If I did, I would oppose it. But I know full well that we must, all of us consumers—the laborers, the business men, the teachers, the children, the rich and the poor, the young and the old, the men and the women—act together to find our way closer and easier and cheaper to the sources of our food supply. And I know full well that the farmers must work together to find their way, by better transportation, better marketing and organized cooperative effort, closer to the consumers of America.

If these two—producers and consumers of food—are not brought closer together by organization, by better railroad service, by the auxiliary of motor-truck facilities, by better roads, by the removal of legal obstructions to organized effort, I know that organized profiteering will squeeze in somewhere between the producer and the consumer.

I do not speak in a sentimental generality when I say this. I hope I am saying something which will not only point the way to a fair and just prosperity for American agriculture and tend to stop land speculation and the increase of the tenant farmer, but which will be one big, practical step taken against the high cost of living. It will be taken in the name of no class, but in the name of the people of America.

Years ago a Chinese philosopher uttered a profound truth when he said: "The well-being of a people is like a tree; agriculture is its root, manufacture and commerce are its branches and its life; if the root is injured the leaves fall, the branches break and the tree dies."

It may seem strange to many good people that at this particular time any one should quote this saying of a wise old Chinese. Never in all our history have prices of farm products ruled so high, measured in dollars, as during the past four years. Farm land in the great surplus-producing states has advanced to unheard-of prices, with every indication that, but for the tight money conditions, it would go still higher. Apparently the farmers of the land are enjoying unprecedented prosperity. Why then, even by implication, suggest that something may be wrong with our agriculture, and that the trouble may be communicated to our manufacturers and commerce? People in the cities are disposed to think that if there is anything wrong it is in the cities where food is selling at such high prices, and not in the country where the food is produced. But both farm and city students of national problems see in the present agricultural situation certain conditions which give cause for real concern to every lover of his country.

An intelligent discussion of our agriculture at the present time must take note of what has happened since the middle of the last century. At that time a fine rural civilization had been built up east of the Mississippi River, with Ohio in the heart of the corn belt and standing in about the same relation to agriculture as Iowa stands to-day. The agricultural frontier had been pushed beyond the Mississippi, and abundant food was being raised to support the growing industrial life of the East.

Then came the civil war, and following it the great western migration into the fertile, open plains of what is now the Central West. Through the homestead law the government gave a farm of the richest land in the world to every man who wanted one. Railroads were built, the prairies were plowed up, and almost over night the agricultural production of the United States increased by fifty per cent. Grains were produced and sold at the bare cost of utilizing the soil, and the farmers of the older states to the east were smothered by this flood of cheap grain. The only thing that could be done with this super-abundance of food was to build cities out of it. And great cities we did build, not only in the United States, but across the seas. The world has never seen, and probably may never again see, such a terrific impulse toward city-building on a vast scale as that which was given by the over-production of farm products during the latter part of the nineteenth century and the first few years of the twentieth.

What are ordinarily dull statistics will strikingly illumine the situation which I have been trying to convey. In the decade from 1900 to 1910 the city population of the United States increased thirty-five per cent, while the rural population increased only eleven per cent. The number of farm utilities probably increased less, but we do know officially that the city population increased more than three times as rapidly as the rural population. The figures are not yet complete for the decade ending with 1920, but sufficient reports have been published to give us a very dependable estimate. The indications are that no increase will be shown in the number of farms and no increase in strictly farm population. In all probability, dating from 1920, we shall estimate our farm population as thirty per cent of the whole while the urban population will make up the other seventy per cent.

Another interesting fact to reveal the danger in changing

conditions: Only a few decades ago, indeed from the very beginning, the exports of the United States were soil-grown or
farm-produced materials. On the other hand, most of our imports were manufactured articles. In the last half century, year
after year the exports of farm-grown products have decreased—
except during the World War—and exports of manufactured
products have increased until again we are rapidly reaching the
zero mark from the standpoint of agricultural supplies to the
world. Each year our imports show larger and larger quantities
of farm-grown products and the time is almost with us when the
imports of farm-grown products will exceed the exports, in
short, when our farm population will not be supplying the products necessary for our own people.

The farmer suffered during this changing period. Over-
production means low prices, and he over-produced with a
vengeance, though it was an inevitable part of the scheme of
American development. He was obliged to practise grinding
economy, and to live as far as possible from the produce of his
own acres. He did live essentially within his own productivity,
and the farm was the factory for the agricultural home. "Land
poor" was a common expression in the farming country. Many,
and especially the ambitious boys, abandoned the farms and
added themselves to the growing population of the cities, driv-
en by the hardships of the farm and attracted by the greater rewards offered by the cities.

By 1905, it was becoming apparent that the consuming power of the cities and industrial centers would soon be large enough
to equalize the producing power of the farms. Prices of farm
products began to advance, and with this advance an increase in
the price of farm land. Improved machinery increased the number of acres one man could farm, thereby decreasing his cost of
production. The expression "farm poor" was no longer heard.
Men who had not secured farms of their own began to seek

them, and the march to the West and Northwest was resumed. Irrigation projects were started and the homestead law made more liberal in order to make the settlement of the semi-arid country more attractive. New areas of government land were opened for entry.

In the meantime, the consuming public had become concerned over the prospect of paying higher prices for foodstuffs. Cities and industrial centers had been built up on ridiculously cheap food; indeed, their building was the first essential in developing farm values. Then the increase in price called for readjustment and required wage advances. Organizations of city business men began to take an interest in farm affairs and preach the duty of increased production. The "Back to the Land" cry began to be heard. Increased appropriations by Congress and by the state legislatures were made to stimulate better methods of farming and thus increase production in hope of keeping down food prices. The rural uplift movement was started with the thought that, by making conditions on the farm more attractive, the drift from the farm to the city might be checked. The work of agricultural colleges was strengthened by the addition of extension departments, the function of which is to take the teaching of better methods of farming and stock-growing into the counties and smaller communities, and especially to stimulate an interest in farming among the boys and girls. All sorts of efforts were made to check the drift from the farm to the city, and to maintain farm production.

In truth, here in America, farming came to that stage where it ceased to be a mere struggle for sustenance, and it found its place amid the competition for achievement. It was no longer the inherently directed operation, with the soil for restricted living, but became a commercial, scientific operation with Mother Nature, to share in the accomplishments of a modern life, and know a participation in modern rewards.

Then came the World War which accelerated the movement which was already under full headway. The cry for food which came from the nations across the sea caused further advances in prices of farm products, as well as in prices of farm land, and both profits and patriotism stimulated production. But with this increased demand for the products of the farm came also an increased demand for the products of our factories and other industrial enterprises, resulting in higher wages, and the city continued to pull from the farm large numbers of young men who did not have farms of their own and could see no prospect of getting them, and who thought they could see in the city better wages and greater opportunities for advancement, as well as more attractive living conditions. If the facts were available it would be found, probably during the period from 1905 to 1917, the time of our entrance into the war, the drift from the farm to the city continued with little abatement notwithstanding the more hopeful conditions on the farm.

The splendid part played by the farmers of the nation during the war probably never will be understood or fully appreciated by our people. More than twenty-five per cent of all our fighting men came from the farms, and after sending their sons to the camps, the fathers and mothers, with the help of the younger children, turned to and produced more food than was ever before produced in the history of the world in the same time and from the same area of land. Their working days were measured not by the clock, but by the number of daylight hours. They took to themselves the responsibility of feeding not only our own people, but also our allies across the sea. In more ways than one, our farmers made the war their war, and counted no sacrifice too great to help fight it through to a successful finish. The story of what they did, written by some one who understands it, will furnish one of the most glorious chapters in American history. One thing I may say—in every American conflict, from the Revolution for independence to the World War for maintained rights, the farmer has been one hundred per cent American and ready for every sacrifice.

Without speaking at length of farm production and prices during the war, it is necessary to note certain results, if we are to deal understandingly with the agricultural situation at the present time, and speak intelligently of a future policy. War conditions put a premium on grain growing at the expense of live stock production. As a consequence, many stock producers and feeders have suffered heavy and, in some cases, ruinous losses. If this condition should continue, we are in danger, in the near future, of having to pay very high prices for our meats.

For two outstanding reasons the maintenance of a normal balance between live stock and grain production is a matter of national concern. One is that we are a meat-eating people, and should have a fairly uniform supply at a reasonable price. Conditions which either greatly stimulate or greatly discourage live stock production result in prices altogether too high for the average consuming public or altogether too low for the producer. The other is that the over-stimulation of grain production depletes the fertility of our land, which is our greatest national asset, and results in a greater supply than can be consumed at a price profitable to the producer, and finally to wide-spread agricultural distress from which all of our people suffer. As a reconstruction measure, therefore, our government should do everything in its power to restore the normal balance between live stock and grain production, and thus encourage the prompt return to that system of diversified farming by which alone we can maintain our soil fertility. This is a matter of immediate importance to all of our people.

No one can forecast with certainty the trend of prices of farm products during the next two or three years. Recovery from a world crisis such as we have experienced is slow, inevitably. It is like the human convalescence from a long and dangerous illness. Our relations with the world-at-large are such that important happenings in other lands have a marked effect upon conditions here at home. Order must be restored, industries rebuilt, devastated lands reclaimed, transportation re-established, the vast armies re-absorbed in the occupations of normal life. The near future promises to be a period of uncertainty for the farmer as well as for the men engaged in industrial enterprises. America has no greater problem than returning securely to the normal, onward road again. This isn't looking backward—it is a forward look to stability and security.

It must be evident, however, to any one who has given the matter even superficial consideration, that we have now come to the end of the long period of agricultural exploitation in the United States. No longer are there great and easy and awaiting areas of fertile land for the land hungry. We have now under the plow practically all of our easily-tillable land, though idle areas await reclamation and development by that genius and determination which ever have made nature respond to human needs. Additions of consequence, which we may make to our farming area from this time on, must come by putting water on the dry lands of the arid and semi-arid country, or by taking water off of the swamp lands, of which we have large areas in some sections, or by digging the stumps out of the cut-over timber lands of the North and South. There are, of course, large possibilities in intensive farming, in that land thrift which admits of neither waste nor neglect, and in ever-improving methods which must be as inspiring to agricultural life as to the professions or to commercial leadership. I want a soul in farming, to set aglow the most independent and self-respecting activity in all the world.

The time has come when, as a nation, we must determine upon a definite agricultural policy. We must decide whether we shall undertake to make of the United States a self-sustaining nation—which means that we shall grow within our own boundaries all of the staple food products needed to maintain the highest type of civilization—or whether we shall continue to exploit our agricultural resources for the benefit of our industrial and commercial life, and leave to posterity the task of finding food enough, by strong-arm methods, if necessary, to support the coming hundreds of millions. I believe in the self-sustaining, independent, self-reliant nation, agriculturally, industrially and politically. We are then the guarantors of our own security and are equal to the task.

If we should unhappily choose the course of industrial and commercial promotion at the expense of agriculture, cities will continue to grow at the expense of the rural community, agriculture will inevitably break down and finally destroy the finest rural civilization with the greatest possibilities the world has ever seen. Decreased farm production will make dear food and we shall be obliged to send our ships to far-away nations in search of cheap foodstuffs the importation of which is sure to intensify agricultural discouragement and distress at home. Ultimately there will come the same fatal break-down and from the same causes, that has destroyed the great civilizations of centuries past.

If, on the other hand, we shall determine to build up here a self-sustaining nation—and what lover of his country can make a different choice?—then we must at once set about the development of a system of agriculture which will enable us to feed our people abundantly, with something to spare for export in years of plenty, and at prices which will insure to the farmer and his family both financial rewards and educational, social and religious living conditions fairly comparable to those offered by the cities. A sound system of agriculture can not be maintained on any other basis. Anything short of a fair return upon invested capital and a fair wage for the labor which goes into the crops, and enough in addition to enable the farmer to maintain the fertility of his soil and insure against natural hazards, will drive large numbers of farmers to the cities.

A frank recognition by all of our people of this fundamental truth is necessary, if we are successfully to work out this great national problem. It is a matter of even greater concern to the people of the cities than to the farmer and the farm community. If we can not by painstaking study and wise statesmanship arrive at such understanding and application of economic laws as will enable us to bring about a fair balance between our urban and rural industries, bringing prosperity to both and permitting neither to fatten at the expense of the other, we can not hope for concord, and without concord there is no assurance for the future.

Heretofore the farmer has been an individualist. Living a somewhat isolated life and being compelled to work long hours, it has not been easy for him to gather with his fellows. He has not had a ready means of defense against the strong organizations of both capital and labor, which in their own interest have at times imposed unfair conditions upon him. It is true that at times, during the past fifty years, there have been temporary farmer organizations brought together to combat some unusually burdensome conditions but usually breaking down when the emergency has passed.

But of late years there have sprung up farmer organizations of a quite different sort—organizations with a very large membership, with an aggressive and intelligent leadership, and with a way of raising whatever funds they may find necessary to promote the interest of their members. The leaders of these organizations are learning rapidly how to adapt to their work the methods which business men and working men have found successful in furthering their own interests. The fruit-growers of the western coast have become so strong that they are now able not only to do away with many of the expenses heretofore paid to others, but also to influence the price of their products. The grain-growers of the West and Northwest have become strong enough to bring about many changes they desired in the marketing of their crops. The farmers of the corn belt states are rapidly perfecting the most powerful organization of farmers ever known in this country. All of these are natural developments in the evolving change of relationship and the modern complexities of productivity and exchange.

It is more than conceivable, it is apparent, that we are able to deal more wisely and more justly with our agriculture than we have in the past. Unless we do deal more fairly there may come a conflict between the organized farmers in the surplus-producing states and those who insist on buying their crops below production costs. We have witnessed the restricted production of manufactures and of labor, but we have not yet experienced the intentionally restricted production of foodstuffs. Let us hope we never may. It is our business to produce and conserve, not to deny, deprive or destroy.

I have no thought of suggesting that the government should work out an elaborate system of agriculture and then try to impose it on the farmers of the country. That would be utterly repugnant to American ideals. Government paternalism, whether applied to agriculture or to any other of our great national industries, would stifle ambition, impair efficiency, lessen production and make us a nation of dependent incompetents. The farmer requires no special favors at the hands of the government. All he needs is a fair chance and just such consideration for agriculture as we ought to give to a basic industry, and ever seek to promote for our common good.

The need of farm representation in larger governmental affairs is recognized. During the past seven years the right of agriculture to a voice in government administration has been practically ignored, and at times the farmer has suffered grievously as a result. The farmer has a vital interest in our trade relations with other countries, in the administration of our financial policies, and in many of the larger activities of the government. His interests must be safeguarded by men who understand his needs, he must be actually and practically represented.

The right of farmers to form cooperative associations for the marketing of their products must be granted. The concert of agriculture is as essential to farms as a similar concert of action is to factories. A prosperous agriculture demands not only efficiency in production, but efficiency in marketing. Through cooperative associations the route between the producer and the consumer can and must be shortened. Wasteful effort can and must be avoided. Unnecessary expense can and must be eliminated. It is to the advantage of all of our people that every possible improvement be made in our methods of getting the products of our farms into the hands of the people who consume them. The legitimate functions of the middleman may continue to be performed, by private enterprise, under conditions where the middleman is necessary and gives his skill to our joint welfare. The parasite in distribution who preys on both producer and consumer must no longer sap the vitality of this fundamental life.

We should have a scientific study of agricultural prices and farm production costs, both at home and abroad, with a view to reducing the frequency of abnormal fluctuations here. Stabilization will contribute to everybody's confidence. Farmers have complained bitterly of the frequent and violent fluctuations in prices of farm products, and especially in prices of live stock. They do not find fluctuations—such fluctuations—in the products of other industries. In a general way prices of farm products must go up or down according to whether there is a plentiful crop or a short one. The farmer's raw materials are the fertility of the soil, the sunshine and the rain; and the size of his crops is measured by the supply of these raw materials and the skill with which he makes use of them. He can not control his production and adjust it to the demand as can the manufacturer. But he can see no good reason why the prices of his products should fluctuate so violently from week to week, and sometimes from day to day. We must get a better understanding of the factors which influence agricultural prices; with a view to avoiding these violent fluctuations and bringing about average prices, which shall bear a reasonable relation to the cost of production. We do not offer any quack remedies in this matter, but we do pledge ourselves to make a thorough study of the disease, find out what causes it, and then apply the remedy which promises a cure.

We promise to put an end to unnecessary price-fixing of farm products and to ill-considered efforts arbitrarily to reduce farm product prices. In times of national crisis, when there is a known scarcity of any necessary product, price control for the purpose of making a fair distribution of the stores on hand may be both necessary and wise. But we know that there can be no repeal of natural laws—the eternal fundamentals. The history of the last three thousand years records the folly of such efforts. If the price of any farm product, for example, is arbitrarily fixed at a point which does not cover the cost of production, the farmer is compelled to reduce the production of that particular crop. This results in a shortage which in turn brings about higher prices than before, and thus intensifies the danger from which it was sought to escape. In times past, many nations have tried to hold down living costs by arbitrarily fixing prices of farm products. All such efforts have failed, and have usually brought national disaster.

Government drives against food prices such as we have experienced during the past two years are equally vain and useless.

The ostensible purpose of such drives is to reduce the price the consumer pays for food. The actual result is unjustly to depress for a time the prices the farmer receives for his grains and live stock, but with no appreciable reduction in the price the consumer pays. Such drives simply give the speculator and the profiteer additional opportunities to add to their exactions, while they add to the uncertainty and discouragement under which the farmer is laboring during this period of readjustment.

We favor the administration of the farm loan act, so as to help men who farm to secure farms of their own, and to give to them long-time credits needed to practise the best methods of diversified farming.

We also favor the authorization of associations to provide the necessary machinery to furnish personal credit to the man, whether land owner or tenant, who is hampered for lack of working capital. The highest type of rural civilization is that in which the land is farmed by the men who own it. Unfortunately, as land increases in value, tenancy also increases.

This has been true throughout history. At the present time probably one-half of the high priced land in the corn belt states is farmed by men, who, because of lack of capital, find it necessary to rent. This increase in tenancy brings with it evils which are a real menace to national welfare. The land owner, especially if he be a speculator who is holding for a profit through an advance in value, is concerned chiefly in securing the highest possible rent. The tenant who lacks sufficient working capital, and who too often is working under a short time lease, is forced to farm the land to the limit and rob it of its fertility in order to pay the rent. Thus we have a sort of conspiracy between landlord and tenant to rob the soil upon which our national well-being and indeed our very existence depend. Amid such conditions, we have inefficient schools, broken-down churches, and a sadly-limited social life. We should, therefore, concern ourselves not only in helping men to secure farms of their own, and in helping the tenant secure the working capital he needs to carry on the best methods of diversified farming, but we should work out a system of land-leasing which, while doing full justice to both landlord and tenant, will at the same time conserve the fertility of the soil.

We do not longer recognize the right to speculative profit in the operation of our transportation systems, but we are pledged to restore them to the highest state of efficiency as quickly as possible. Agriculture has suffered more severely than any other industry through the inefficient railroad service of the last two years. Many farmers have incurred disastrous losses through inability to market their grain and live stock. Such a condition must not be permitted to continue. We must bring about conditions which will give us prompt service at the lowest possible rates.

We need a revision of the tariff as soon as conditions shall make it necessary for the preservation of the home market for American labor, American agriculture and American industry. For a permanent good fortune all must have a common interest. If we are to build up a self-sustaining agriculture here at home, the farmer must be protected from unfair competition from those countries where agriculture is still being exploited and where the standards of living on the farm are much lower than here. We have asked for higher American standards, let us maintain them.

The farmers of the corn belt, for example, are already threatened with unfair competition from the Argentine, whose rich soil is being exploited in heedless fashion and where the renters who farm it are living under conditions more miserable than the poorest tenants in the United States. In times past, duties on agricultural products were largely in the nature of paper tariffs, for we were a great surplus-producing nation. Now that consumption at home is so nearly reaching normal production, the American farmer has a right to insist that in our trade relations with other countries he shall have the same consideration that is accorded to other industries, and we mean to protect them all.

So long as America can produce the foods we need, I am in favor of buying from America first. It is this very preference which impels development and improvement. Whenever America can manufacture to meet American needs—and there is almost no limit to our genius and resources—I favor producing in America first. I commend American preference for American productive activities, because material good fortune is essential to our higher attainment, and linked indissolubly are farm and factory in the economic fabric of American life.

Under a sound system of agriculture, fostered and safeguarded by wise and fair administration of state and federal government, the farmers of the United States can feed our people for many centuries—perhaps indefinitely. But we must understand conditions, and make a new appraisal of relationships, and square our actions to the great underlying foundation of all human endeavor. Farming is not an auxiliary, it is the main plant, and geared with it, inseparably, is every wheel of transportation and industry. America could not go on with a dissatisfied farming people, and no nation is secure where land-hunger abides. We need fewer land-hogs who menace our future, and more fat hogs for ham and bacon. We need less beguilement in cultivating a quadrennial crop of votes and more consideration for farming as our basic industry. We need less appeal to class consciousness, and more resolute intelligence in promptly solving our problems. We need rest and recuperation for a soil which has been worked out in agitation, and more and better harvests in the inviting fields of mutual understanding. We need less of grief about the ills which we may charge to the neglect of our own citizenship, and more confidence in just government, along with determination to make and hold it just.

We need to contemplate the miracle of America in that understanding which enables us to appreciate that which made us what we are, and then resolve to cling fast to all that is good and go confidently on to great things.

We need to recall that America and its triumphs are not a gift to the world through a paralyzing internationality, but the glories of the Republic are the fruits of our nationality and its inspirations—of freedom, of opportunity, of equal rights under the Constitution, of Columbia offering the cup of American liberty to men thirsting to achieve and beckoning men to drink of the waters of our political life and be rewarded as they merit it. I think that the paths which brought us to the point where the world leadership might have been ours—as it might have been in 1919—in the first century and a third of national life, ought to be the way to the answered aspirations of this great Republic. I like to turn for reflection sometimes, because I get therein the needed assurance for the onward march of the morrow. To-day we have contemplated American farming in the broadest possible way, have been reminded where we have been remiss; tomorrow we want to greet farmers of America in the freedom and fulness of farming productivity, impelled by the assurance that they are to have their full part in the rewards of righteous American activity.

WHAT OF OUR CHILDREN
A Message for Mothers

In my address to women voters last October, I spoke of my desire that there should be created in our government a department of public welfare. It is with some satisfaction that I am now able to say that since the election I have had opportunity to discuss that proposal with a number of leaders of liberal public thought in and out of Congress, with reference to crystallizing it into legislative accomplishment, and have found them eager to help in the constructive task.

Its accomplishment will tardily place our government on something like an equal footing with governments which have long maintained ministries of education represented in their Cabinets. While my own ideal envisages a broader scope for the new department, giving it concern with many other phases of human welfare, it is interesting to know that its creation will for the first time place this great work on a phase of dignity comparable to that given it in many other countries.

Whether we may esteem it wise or unwise, the modern mother must realize that society is disposed more and more to take from her control the training, the intellectual direction and the spiritual guidance of her children. We may well plead with the mothers to make the most for good, of the lessened opportunity they possess for molding the lives and minds of their children. Through such cooperative effort as this is, it seems to me, there is opportunity for a great service. Herein is presented the opportunity to lift up the poorer and the less fortunate to a higher level.

The mother who indefatigably seeks to train her own children rightly will be performing this service not only for her own children, but for those from other homes not so richly blessed with the finer things of life. I confess to no great satisfaction in the good fortune of those families, which, when they become sufficiently well to do, like to take their children away from the public schools and give them the doubtful advantage of more exclusive educational processes. I like the democracy of the community school and, indeed, I would like to see a greater measure of it enforced in the public schools by the elimination of those evidences of extravagance in dress and social indulgence which make for the development of something like caste within our democracy.

On the side of the teacher and the responsible authorities back of her, there must be the same ready disposition to cooperate with the home and the mother. Our public school system leaves to the home and its influence the great duty of instilling into the child those fundamental concepts of religion which are so essential in shaping the character of individual citizens, and, therefore, of the nation. That duty remains to be performed at the hearthside and will always be a peculiar prerogative of the mother. I could wish, indeed, that our nation might have a revival of religious spirit along these lines. There never was a time when the world stood in more need than it does now of the consolations and reassurances which only a firm religious faith can have. It is a time of uncertainty, of weakened faith in the efficiency of institutions, of industrial systems, of economic hypothesis, of dictum and dogma. Whatever our realm, let not our engrossment with those things which are concerned merely with matter and mind distract from proper attention to those which are of the spirit and the soul.

It has been demonstrated to astonishing and alarming certainty that a large proportion of school children and even of adults suffer from under-nourishment. Perhaps in the case of most adults the fault is of the individual rather than society. With children, however, it is otherwise. If society has permitted the development of a system under which the citizens of to-morrow suffer real privation to-day, then the obligation is upon society to right that wrong, to insure some measure of justice to the children, who are not responsible for being here.

I am not of those who believe legislation can find panaceas for all ills, but on the other hand I am not of those who fear to undertake through legislation the formulation of new programs.

I firmly believe that our country, along with others that claim a share in the world's leadership, has lately achieved one victory in behalf of a better understanding and more intelligent grasp of these problems. I refer to the bestowal upon women of full participation in the privileges and obligations of citizenship. With her large part wider in influence in the world of affairs, I think we shall see woman and her finer spiritual instincts at length leading mankind to higher planes of religion, of humanism and of ennobling spirituality.

Healthful mothers amid fit conditions for maternity, healthful, abundantly nourished children amid fit conditions for development mentally and physically—all made certain by the generation of to-day in its concern for to-morrow, will guarantee a citizenship from the soil of America which will be the guarantee of American security and the American fulfillment.

THE PRESS AND THE PUBLIC

A Message for Newspapermen

The passing years have wrought great changes in the newspaper business even in the comparatively short time since my adventurous entry upon it. The prolific inventors of printing machinery and other appliances have borne their share in it; the free rural delivery, the advance in education bringing new multitudes of readers, have all had their influence in the developments and evolutions which have followed. I can remember when in most of the county-seat towns the possession by one of the papers of a power-press,—even if the power was applied by a husky man attached to a cranked wheel,—was widely proclaimed as an evidence of astounding prosperity and recognized as a potential influence.

We have seen the type-setting machines come in—not to supplant the hand compositor, but to shift him to the "Ad. Alleys" and the job cases. They have taught the printers, as the mowers and reapers have taught the farmers, that increased capacity in production does not mean a lessening of a demand for labor, but on the contrary increased production, through increased efficiency, mental, manual or mechanical, opens new avenues for employment and brings luxuries into the class of common commodities.

The diminished numbers of country weekly publications came in the extension of the rural delivery mail carriers. We learned that the farmer who got his mail every morning at his front door would not wait a week or even two or three days for his newspaper. He learned, too, what market reports meant to him. Machinery had lightened his toil and shortened his hours, except seasonably, and he had time to read and the desire to be informed. The telephones had brought him in touch with some news centers and he heard hints which he wanted confirmed. Electricity lighted many farm-houses and lengthened the reading period.

The rural delivery with the parcel post also wiped out many of the cross-roads stores where the rural dweller was wont to gather for neighborly gossip and discussion of great events, and this, too, had its influence in broadening the demand for the daily paper.

Another change was brought about by two causes. In the days of thirty or forty years ago, there was a bitterness and acerbity about political discussion which caused the factional newspaper to multiply if not to flourish. It was not difficult to start a newspaper in those days. A very small amount of cash and a little credit would procure a modest plant, and another journal would be "established" to fight its owner's quarrels and divide the limited patronage of its limited field.

But now it costs real money to equip a newspaper plant—to install linotype machines, fast presses and type in quantities, and it costs a "fortune" to buy news print. The "high cost of printing" has had its way with us and we find fewer but generally better newspapers than we had in the Ohio counties when our population was half what it is now.

The changes have been great, but I question whether they have all been in the nature of improvements. The old-time paper—going back to the last half of last century—was usually a real journal of opinion. It reflected the convictions as well as the opinions of its owner and editor, and it was a real molder of opinion in its influence upon its readers and the community it served. The editors were not always great writers, but they were generally patriots, and honestly desirous to render service. And they were generally partisan and they preached party gospel and believed in it. Sometimes it seems to me that the transition from the party organ to the "independent" newspaper, so-called, has not been an unmixed blessing. The partisan newspaper, in its editorial expression, uttered the considered views of a large element of our citizenship, while the "independent" paper is often the organ solely of its owner, or it is colorlessly neutral.

There is a temptation to blend shop talk with politics, because I know how intimately newspaper men are thinking of the problem of news print, the cost of which has added so excessively to the expense account of every newspaper. Men speak of immediate relief, but the problem is too big for that.

Permanent and ample relief must come by going to the underlying causes. No forest consumption like ours can go on indefinitely without imperiling our pulpwood supply. Competent authority tells us that the pulpwood in New York State will be exhausted in ten years, that New England will be denuded of its supply in twenty years. Our needs are so vast that we imported nearly one and a half million tons of pulpwood from Canada in 1918, and the Canadian price advanced from ten to twenty-five dollars per cord. It is obvious that we must have a forest policy which shall make us self-reliant once more. We ought to be looking ahead to produce our timber for our pulpwood needs and also our timber for our lumber needs. Forest conservation is a necessary accompaniment to printing expansion, and a matter of common concern to all the people.

Three-fifths of the original timber in this country is gone, and there are eighty million idle acres in which we ought to be growing forests for the future. Planning for the future, with added protection of our present forests from fire, is a matter of deep concern to publishers in particular, but to all of constructive America as well.

But I want to turn your thoughts to a service in the columns. There is one service for the American press, not partisan but patriotic, for which there is a call to-day such as we have never known before. America needs a baptism in righteousness and a new consecration in morality.

It was stated the other day that a reflex of the war has been so revealed in broken obligations and betrayed trusts that the bonding companies are called upon to meet such losses that the whole schedule for fidelity policies must be rewritten. If my information is correct, the security companies have never been called upon to meet so many and such heavy losses in all the history of that business.

Probably the betrayals of trust, the smaller ones at least, are in part due to the high cost of living, and the failure of salary scales to respond to the new demands of the salaried working forces. Many instances are reported, however, where salaries were ample to meet even extravagant practises, and the sums stolen were beyond all limits which might attend living costs. The conclusion is forced that it is a reflex of the moral degeneracy of war, of the barbarity and cunning, and ruthlessness and greed in war's aftermath.

There was so much of extravagance, so much of waste, so much of needless expenditures in seeking for speed in war preparation, that the government often was robbed without scruple of conscience, often without hindrance. It is not surprising to find a reflex in offices and counting rooms.

Call it reaction if you like, we need the old standards of honesty, the lofty standards of fidelity. If I could call for but one distinction, I would like ours to be known as an honest people. We need the stamp of common, every-day honesty, everywhere. We need it in business, we need it in labor, we need it in professions, in pulpits, in editorial rooms, in circulation count. Aye, we need it in politics, in government, in our daily lives. Dishonesty and corruption had more to do with the Russian revolution than all the cruelty of autocracy.

If governments and their diplomats in Europe had been honest, there would have been no war. If everybody concerned had been rigidly honest, peace might have followed the armistice within ninety days. If we could only be genuinely honest with one another, we could put an end to industrial and social unrest, and if we were only honest with God, we would become a moral and religious people again.

I suppose some people will say I am "looking backward." But if we may look backward to clear our vision we may look forward more confidently, and lift our gaze above and beyond the sordid and selfish things and the baser side of life so horridly revealed when passions are aflame. There is sure progress for a simple-living, reverent people, fearing God and loving righteousness. It is good to look back to make sure of the way religious mothers taught and then face the front with renewed faith.

If we are living in the past to recall the wisdom of Washington, the equal rights of Jefferson, the genius of Hamilton, the philosophy of Franklin, or the sturdiness of Jackson; if it is looking backward to recall the sympathy and steadfastness of Lincoln, the restoration of McKinley or the awakening by Roosevelt, I am happy to drink of the past for my inspiration for the morrow.

Engineering is a scientific pursuit and a very accurate one. It has been my fortune to witness some railway surveys, and I never knew an engineer who did not turn his transit to his backsight to make sure of his line by which we were to move on. We are thinking to-day of the route by which America is to go on. The past is secure, and I would like to project our future course on the security of the past.

Something has been said lately about looking to the sunrise of to-morrow, not the sky-line of the setting sun. Every hope in life is of to-morrow, we could not live yesterdays again if we would. But the glory of ten thousand morrows was wrought in the wisdom gleaned on yesterday. Mariners and planters and harvesters—all study the sky. Sometimes above the sky-line, in lands where the desert stretches, there is the mirage, with its lure to the fevered and thirsting, with inviting promise of relief. It has speeded travel and revived hopes, and spurned waning strength, it has diverted from proved routes, and left death and destruction as its monument to broken promises. In the horizon of maintained constitutionalism, there is no mirage to lure the American caravan, but we mean to go securely on, over the proved routes of triumph for the republic and the people thereof.

No one agency can render a greater service in holding to the charted way than a conscientious and patriotic American press. But it must remain free, utterly free; along with freedom of speech, freedom of religious belief, and the freedom of righteous pursuit, it must be honest and it must be rejoicing in American nationality which is our priceless possession.

VII

THE THEATER
A Message for Actors

Whether one contemplates the present-day stage in deference to its part in art or its vast opportunities for educational work or its commercial importance, it is really a very significant factor in the activities, progress and attainment of our common country. I presume many had rather be estimated from the purely professional side as devotees of a very great and appealing art. It is very easy, on the other hand, for the practical mind to be impressed by the fact that the United States of America expends approximately one billion dollars per year for its amusement on the stage. Perhaps nothing more significantly reflects the changed condition of living or the ability of our people to indulge in those things which are counted a necessary part of the fuller modern life.

There is another phase, however, which is even more appealing to me. I do not in any way minimize my high regard for the great art involved in the splendid work of the spoken drama or the musical stage, but the coming of the silent drama has revealed to us an agency for education which no human being could have reasonably conceived a quarter of a century ago. We have no single avenue for the dissemination of information equal to that of the moving picture. I do not know that any one now has an approximate measure of the possibilities which may come. Pictures are very convincing things. I confess that sometimes the camera fools us more or less, but, as a general proposition, it is a very dependable agency of the truth, and it has the facility for conveying essential educational truths to the remotest parts of the world.

Nothing is more remarkable than the enlarged enjoyment of the drama through picture distribution. It is only a few years ago that the rural community saw very little of the drama and much of what it saw was not to be taken as a very creditable example of the best in dramatic art. Most artists have a very strong aversion to what is properly known as barnstorming, and really worth-while stage entertainment was a very rare thing in the rural communities. Many of us had examples of home production in which we yielded to a very natural inclination to act some part. This manifestation is one which we developed rather unconsciously from the earliest days in the public schools. The recitation or the declamation, so frequently employed by schooling youths and encouraged in every home, is only one of the early tendencies of the dramatic art.

I will not venture to recall my recollections of the amateur stage and the home production, or any part I had therein, but I do recall that out of the atmosphere of the small town stage has come many a star to illumine the theatrical world. It has seemed to me that there are two elemental essentials to the inauguration of a dramatic career: one is native talent and the other is opportunity for its development. With these, of course, must be ambition and determination, because there is no eminence attained in human life without these. It is befitting to recall that no actor or actress ever wrought an abiding triumph on any stage, without knowing the soul of the character enacted, and we Americans, to enact our part in the drama of world civilization, must know the soul of America, and play the part of real Americans.

If it will not seem out of place, I want to convey one message to the associates in the various activities of the stage world. I think we have been making noble progress in the attainment of high quality and the elevation of standards. I would like the American stage to be like American citizenship, the best in all the world. I think the inspiration for success lies in ever lifting the standards higher and higher. It is extremely necessary to continue to elevate the standards of the silent drama, because we send the picture stage to all the people of the United States and it is of common concern that its influence must be the very best. I do not think a people can be fortunate with various standards of censorship. I presume censorship is very essential, but I do not think we require one standard for one locality and another standard for another. We must ever be on guard against debasement for momentary gain, on the one hand, and against narrow exaction which destroys the artistic merit of a production and the real lesson intended, on the other. However, there is nothing so essential to the highest art that it need be offensive to becoming public morals.

Without venturing to quote the very familiar reference to all the world as a stage, I have been thinking lately that there is a great likeness between political life under popular government and many of our most successful productions on the stage. Some of the most impressive plays I have ever witnessed have been those where all that interest is not riveted in the lead. For example, in the production of *Julius Caesar,* which attracted the attention of much of the foremost talent of the stage, one great actor would choose to portray the character of Cassius, another may have elected to play the part of Brutus, still another thought to assume the role of Caesar himself. The work of the lead was not transcendent, but the effectiveness of the play was dependent on the perfection with which every character was present-ed. To my mind it is the ideal spoken production where each one plays his part with soul and enthusiasm, no matter how insignificant the part may be, so that out of the grouped endeavor comes the perfect offering.

There is an element in every production quite as essential in the modern production as the acting caste, which must work with spirit and devotion and which the public never sees. I refer to the forces behind the scenes, who dress the picture for either spoken or silent drama. I do not assume to mention all elements essential to the modern stage, but I do want to remind the public that on the stage, as in life, are ever the faithful and the tireless without whom we could not accomplish, but who themselves rarely appear on the stage. Their applause must come in the soul of their work and the consciousness of things well done.

There are many plays especially written for notable stars and their presentation has depended on the work of one portraying genius. There is, of course, a fascination in the one-lead drama, but it makes the spectator very much dependent upon one individuality, and if the star should be incapacitated for any reason, there is inevitable disappointment. I think it is a very practical thing to suggest that our American popular government ought not to be a one-lead or a one-star drama of modern civilization. I want to commend the policy of each and every one having his part to play, and we all must play with enthusiasm in order to perfect the whole production. For the supreme offering, we need the all-star cast, presenting America to all the world.

Running over in my mind some of my recollections of the stage, I recall two plays, the production of which left an impress that I shall never forget, especially in their bearing on the present state of human affairs. In one, Forbes Robertson played the leading rôle—*The Passing of the Third Floor Back.* The Stranger in the play urged upon a discordant, suspicious boarding-house family, the gospel of simplicity and honesty and understanding. With a rare sympathy and great patience, and with wholesome good sense and a fine example in himself, he transformed the household and planted happiness where discord had flourished, and rended hypocrisy, and put an end to cheating, and drove snobbery out, and set the flowers of fellowship abloom. We need the lesson this Stranger taught, in our American lives and throughout the world. His was no radical teaching, his was not a highly dramatic or sensational example, there really was not a very striking "punch" in a thing that he said, but the Stranger was soothing and helpful and encouraging and uplifting, and he left sunshine where the shadows of gloom had darkened, and he did it all through sympathy and understanding. He uncovered reality and put pretense aside.

The other play was one of Mansfield's superb productions—*Henry V,* if my memory is correct. I particularly recall a camp scene on the night before a crucial battle, and as I recall it now the King put aside his regal garb, and clad as a simple soldier went among his armed forces to learn their feelings, their confidence, and their fears, and ascertained on terms of equality and intimacy, what a monarch might never have learned in any other way. And he found that the heart of his army was right. He asked concerning the morrow and he found the confidence of the rank and file to be the assurance of a King, and together they fought in triumph the next day.

There is no kingship in this Republic, but thoughtful Americans are wondering about the morrow. Is our civilization secure? It is well to know what is in the hearts of men and women, who are gathered before the camp-fires of human progress. There is a memory of yesterday, the horizon of to-day, and the new hope of to-morrow. Every normal human being wishes for a better morrow than to-day. Every parent in America wishes for his son or daughter all that he inherited, and more. That is why humanity is ever an advancing procession.

But no sane man ever puts aside an assurance of experience for the promise of more experiment. The world can not be stabilized on dreams, but can be steadied by evident truths. It is perfectly normal humanity which delights in a new sensation. One can only pity a people which becomes blasé. It is better to be simple than surfeited. The new thrill is sought on the stage and is sought everywhere in human life. Some of our people lately have been wishing to become "citizens of the world." Not so long since I met a fine elderly daughter of Virginia, who would have been justified in boasting her origin in the Old Dominion and uttering her American pride, but I was shocked to hear her say, "I am no longer an American, I am a citizen of the world." Frankly, I am not so universal, I rejoice to be an American and love the name, the land, the people and the flag.

VIII
AMERICAN EDUCATION
A Message for Teachers

My mind runs back to something like thirty-eight years ago when I was in attendance as a teacher at a Marion County Institute. I had come from college only the year before, and I did what was very much the practise of that time—turned to teaching in my abundant fulness of knowledge, merely as a temporary occupation.

It is a very inspiring thing to be a teacher of American youth. In our modern life we have shifted some of the responsibility which I think should accrue to parenthood over to the teachers in our public schools. So school-teachers have much to do with making the citizenship in this Republic of ours, and they ought to be the best rated profession, the best cared for profession in America. I believe that our teachers should be compensated as liberally, if not more liberally, than any other profession. I do not try to give you the impression that the federal government can do that; but we do have a Federal Bureau of Education which has only a relative influence on educational work. Some day we may have a much larger and more important Department of Education; but in any event the federal government can exert its influence in behalf of a becoming recognition of the teaching profession.

I do not believe that all which has been placed on the shoulders of our teachers ought to be taken from the American homes. I will not discuss that at length, but I do think teachers ought to know the home a little more intimately, and ought to have the cooperation of the parents and the home.

I am not sure I was a very good teacher, but I was at least ambitious to be a good one. I taught in a country school. If you have never done that you don't know the real pleasure of teaching. We had all the branches of elementary teaching, up to the heights of algebra and general history. One day I put on the blackboard the forms for addressing and closing a letter. After explanations, I erased the blackboard form and asked the pupils to address me a letter on their slates. One obstinate youth refused, and I was obliged to discipline him. He happened to be a son of one of the school directors who compensated me for my unusual interest in his boy by writing me that I was engaged to teach what was in the textbook, namely, reading, writing, and arithmetic, and not to go beyond. So he declined to sign my pay warrant! That actually happened only about thirty-eight years ago.

Our teachers represent the great army of those patient soldiers in the cause of humanity upon whom rests one of the most profound responsibilities given to any man or woman. And yet the disadvantages that beset their profession indicate a serious menace to our national institutions. It is, indeed, a crisis in American education that confronts us. If we continue to allow our public instructors to struggle with beggarly wages we shall find ourselves with closed schools; our education will languish and fail. It is a patent fact that never have our teachers, as a whole, been properly compensated. From the days when the country teachers "boarded around" to the present hour the profession has never been adequately compensated. Requiring, as it does, a high degree of mental equipment, a long preparation, severe examination tests, the maintenance of a proper state in society, and giving employment only a part of the year, with compensation too meager, the wonder of it is that we have had the service of these devoted persons employed in educating our youth.

I have a personal recollection of the old-time estimate of school teaching, because I taught one session of district school. For the autumn months I received twenty dollars per month, for the winter double the price, not that I taught better or more, but probably because I built the fires and had more sweeping to do. But then, and earlier, teaching was not a life profession, but rather a resort to youth's temporary earnings, to help prepare for something else. To-day teaching is a life work, a great profession, a life offering on the altar of American advancement.

Education is recognized in our organic law, but it did not need that declaration. America's greatness, her liberty, and her happiness are founded upon her intelligence. They are founded upon that wide dissemination of knowledge which comes only to the many through our educational system.

This subject touches every individual in America. All of us are concerned in our common schools. We ought to be as interested in our teacher's pay as we are in our own. We can't be confident of our schools unless we are confident of our teachers and know they are the best that a great work may command.

Whatever the cause may be for failure to recognize the value of the teacher, measured in wages, it is a lamentable fact that the teacher has done his patient service improperly rewarded through all the years. The burdens of the teachers have increased, greater exactions as to fitness have been imposed, the cost of living has gone up, but we have failed to meet the change.

We have now reached a crisis, when it is imperative that something must be done. I know with what difficulty our public schools have been operated during the past two or three years. Teachers have left the schools for more promising employments and their places have been left unfilled with new enlistments. This condition is not only fatal if continued, but it reflects discredit upon every citizen who has not demanded correction of the evil. We make drafts upon our public treasuries, we are taxed, sometimes unnecessarily, for almost every other conceivable purpose. Let us support adequately the standards of our schools. Let all Americans recognize the necessity and determine upon relief. When the facts are known, America and Americans will respond.

It is fair to say that the federal government is not responsible and can not assume to trespass, but it can give of its influence, it can point out the peril which ought to be clearly evident to every community, it can emphasize the present crisis and make an unfailing call for the educational preparedness for citizenship which is so essential to our continued triumphs.

It is a rather curious indication of the trend toward federal control that at this very moment not less than four or five new Cabinet officers are being proposed—and not without argument, let me say. Some feel there should be a reorganization of the Department of the Interior,—they want to create this and that—and not without reason, too, because it has become a tremendous government within itself. There is one call for a department of engineering—another for a department of health, and thus I might run on. I can not pretend to say to you what ought to be done in each instance, but I can say that I am concerned just as deeply as you are respecting this question of bringing American education up to the very highest standard.

IX

THE IMMIGRANT
A Message for Citizens of Foreign Birth

You who are men and women of foreign birth, I do not address as men and women of foreign birth; I address you as Americans, and through you I would like to reach all the American people. I have no message for you which is not addressed to all the American people, and, indeed, I would consider it a breach of courtesy to you and a breach of my duty to address myself to any group or special interest or to any class or race or creed. We are all Americans, and all true Americans will say, as I say, "America First!"

Let us all pray that America shall never become divided into classes and shall never feel the menace of hyphenated citizenship! Our uppermost thought to-day comes of the awakening which the World War gave us. We had developed the great American Republic; we had become rich and powerful, but we had neglected the American soul. When the war clouds darkened Europe and the storm threatened our own country, we found America torn with conflicting sympathies and prejudices. They were not unnatural; indeed they were, in many cases, very excusable, because we had not promoted the American spirit; we had not insisted upon full and unalterable consecration to our own country—our country by birth or adoption. We talked of the American melting pot over the fires of freedom, but we did not apply that fierce flame of patriotic devotion needed to fuse all into the pure metal of Americanism.

I do not blame the foreign born. Charge it to American neglect. We proclaimed our liberty, but did not emphasize the essentials to its preservation. We boasted our nationality, but we did not magnify the one great spirit essential to perfect national life.

I speak for the fullest American devotion; not in putting aside all the tenderer and dearer attributes of the human heart, but in the consecrations of citizenship. It is not possible, and it ought not to be expected, that Americans of foreign birth shall stifle love for kinsfolk in the lands from which they came. It would be a poor material for the making of an American if one of foreign birth would, or could, be insensible to the fortunes of father and mother, or grandfathers and grandmothers, of brothers and sisters; if he could be insensible to the fortunes of the people from whom he came. America does not want, and does not ask that. We want the finer attributes of humanity in all our citizenship, and we wish these lovable traits in foreign-born and American-born. But we do ask all to think of "America First"; to serve "America First," to defend "America First," and plight an unalterable faith in "America First."

We are unalterably against any present or future hyphenated Americanism. We have put an end to prefixes. The way to unite and blend foreign blood in the life stream of America is to put an end to groups; an end to classes; an end to special appeal to any of them; an end to particular favor for any of them. Let's fix our gaze afresh on the Constitution, with equal rights to all, and put an end to special favors at home and special influence abroad, and think of the American, erect and confident in the rights of his citizenship.

I like to think of an America without sectional lines, an America without class groups. I do not mean the natural fellowship or fraternity, that association which comes from wholesome human traits. I am thinking of the selfish grouping that made us sectional, and the selfish grouping which makes for classes, and the selfish grouping which looks to government to promote selfish ends rather than the good of our common country.

I like to think of an America where every citizen's pride in power and resources, in influence and progress, is founded on what can be done for our people, all our people; not what we may accomplish to the political or national advantage of this or that people in distant lands.

It was my official duty to sit with the Senate Committee on Foreign Relations when it was hearing the American spokesmen for foreign peoples, during the peace conference at Paris. Under the rules, we could give hearing only to Americans, though many whom we had no right to hear sought to bring their appeal to the Senate, as though it possessed some sense of justice which had no voice in Paris. We heard the impassioned appeals of Americans of foreign birth on behalf of the lands from which they came—where their kinsfolk resided. No one doubted their sincerity; no one questioned their right to be interested. But for me there was a foreboding, a growing sense of apprehension.

How can we have American concord; how can we expect American unity; how can we escape strife, if we in America attempt to meddle in the affairs of Europe and Asia and Africa; if we assume to settle boundaries; if we attempt to end the rivalries and jealousies of centuries of Old World strife? It is not alone the menace which lies in involvement abroad; it is the greater danger which lies in conflict among adopted Americans.

This is the objection to the foreign policy attempted, not with the advice and consent of the Senate, but in spite of warning informally uttered. America wants the good will of foreign peoples, and it does not want the ill will of foreign-born who have come to dwell among us.

Nothing helpful has come from the wilful assumption to direct the affairs of Europe. No good of any kind has proceeded from such meddling in Russia. None in the case of Poland. None in the case of the Balkan States. None in the case of Fiume. On the contrary, the mistaken policy of interference has broken the draw-strings of good sense and spilled bad counsel and bad manners all over the world.

That policy, my countrymen, is a bad policy. It is bad enough abroad, but it is even more menacing at home. Meddling abroad tends to make Americans forget that they are Americans. It tends to arouse the old and bitter feelings of race, or former nationality, or foreign ancestry, in the hearts of those who ought never to be forced to turn their hearts away from undivided loyalty and interest given to "America First."

I want America on guard against that course which naturally tends to array Americans against one another. I do not know whether or not Washington foresaw this menace when he warned us against entangling alliances and meddling abroad, but I see it, and I say to you that all America must stand firm against this dangerous and destructive and un-American policy. Meddling is not only dangerous to us, because it leads us into the entanglements against which Washington warned us but it also threatens an America divided in her own household, and tends to drive into groups seeking to make themselves felt in our political life, men and women whose hearts are led away from "America First" to "Hyphen First!"

For Americans who love America, I sound a warning. The time might come when a group or groups of men and women of foreign birth or foreign parentage, not organized for the interest of America, but organized around a resentment against our government interference abroad in their land of origin, might press, by propaganda and political hyphenism, upon our government to serve their own interests rather than the interests of all America. It is not beyond possibility that the day might come—and may God forbid it!—when an organized hyphenated vote in American politics might have the balance of voting power to elect our government. If this were true, America would be delivered out of the hands of her citizenship, and her control might be transferred to a foreign capital abroad.

I address this warning to you because though it is a message to all Americans which you may spread widecast, nevertheless it is of even greater concern to you, who were born on other soil, or whose parents were born upon other soil, then it is to any one else in all the world. America is peculiarly your America. Men and women of foreign blood, indeed, are Americans. They have come here because, under our Republic, grown upon a firm foundation, there is liberty, and the light of democracy which shines in the hearts of all mankind. America is yours to preserve, not as a land of groups and classes, races and creeds, but America, the ONE America! the United States, "America the Everlasting!"

Let us all remember, however, that "America First" does not mean that the America which we all love and under whose flag we must always remain a people united is to be an America blind to the welfare of humanity throughout the world or deaf to the call of world civilization. But our ability to be helpful to mankind and our preparation for leadership lies in first being secure at home, and mighty in our citizenship. Therein lies strength; therein is the source of helpful example.

Let us say it to native-born and to foreign-born—our citizenship ought to be founded first upon our sense of service; we must not be deluded by the idea that government is a magic source of benevolence. No government can ever give out more resources than its citizens put in. Just as good citizenship, whatever its creed, or race, means "America First," so also good government means the welfare of all its citizens.

I insist that American conscience recognize the duty of protecting our national health. I insist that it protect American motherhood, and American childhood, and the American home. I insist that it place the welfare of the human being above all else. I insist that it act, not only to give the weak, and those who need protection, and who righteously should have social justice, their due, but because the concern for the less fortunate is an interest of us all.

Above all, we must give our attention as a nation, to American childhood, because American childhood is the future citizenship of America.

Health comes first. The war disclosed that between a fourth and a third of our young men in the draft were physically delinquent. Examination of our school children in various cities discloses that nearly fifty per cent of them—boys and girls—have physical defects, most of which can be remedied if discovered in time. I do not discuss at the moment the relation of federal health agencies to local health agencies, but I do say that we must insist upon an American conscience acting at once to raise our health standards, especially as they bear upon the welfare of American childhood.

There can be no defense for working conditions which rob the American child of its rights, just as there can be no defense of an industrial life of a nation or the agricultural life of a nation which so draws away the strength of our women that it poisons and weakens motherhood. When we make these assertions of national conscience, we do not make them for political gain, but we make them as a principle standing above party, and as an American principle and in behalf of all America.

It is impossible, my countrymen, to have an America such as we would have her, until there are no failures upon her part to protect American childhood and American motherhood. The nation, the several states and all their communities and all citizens of America must unite to prevent the growth in America of sore spots where the equal opportunity of every man, woman and child to prove his own worth might be taken away from the human individual.

It has seemed fitting to speak of this matter of social betterment, because the greater proportion of our foreign-born Americans have preferred our cities and the lure of the factory to the call of the American farm. It is not surprising. For association's sake, many of them have accepted crowded tenements and privations, and dwelt amid conditions which do not permit standing out in the fulness of American opportunity or measuring to ideal American standards. We want them to know the best America and give their best to America, and in clasping the hand of American conscience and freedom, they shall be impelled to give America both head and heart in that love and loyalty that make in America a people distinct from all others in surpassing love of country.

CONSERVATION AND DEVELOPMENT
A Message for the Mountain West

What a wonderful land is ours! No one has ever come to a full realization of the incomparableness of these United States. Nature has been very generous with her bounty and has given us, in the great and measureless West, a variegated and picturesque empire as beautiful as Switzerland, multiplied many times over in extent, and with a diversification of industry and enterprise which Switzerland could not develop because her mountains are well nigh barren of the riches which characterize the Rockies and the Coast ranges.

Some day, perhaps, we shall come to an appraisal of the mountain West and shall learn something about its contents in coal, copper, iron, gold and silver, and almost every useful mineral deposit; but these are not all; because the mountain West is rich in forests, and lakes of potash, and vast deposits of phosphates, and possesses almost measureless areas that need only water to make them blossom like a garden of Eden; and the water is available and needs only the genius and the courage and capacity of man to apply it practically. People of the United States contemplate the wonderful West from varying viewpoints. In the East, the tendency is to think of it only as a wonderland, but those of the West, who have seen it from the intimate view-point, not only find unbounded interest in its possibilities, but want to sense the pride in its development.

We have come to an era when further development, attended by both reclamation and conservation, which go hand in hand, is an important and urgent problem. The world has always had a struggle to provide its food. In the practical development of the United States, we must ever continue the enlargement of the available food supply. Industrial development in the cities and agricultural development have gone more or less in harmony, because the one is absolutely essential to the other. Basically, we must be sure of our food supply first. The development of the Mississippi Basin was contemporaneous with the development of our wonderful American cities, and the marvel of American development began immediately after the Civil War. In that conflict we made certain of indissoluble union and put an end to all doubts in the Federal Constitution and then turned to expanded settlement and development with full confidence in the future.

When the Union armies were dispersed, farms in the West were made available to tens of thousands of the defenders of union and nationality, the central plains were awaiting, almost untouched, and out of them were builded a dozen splendid commonwealths. There is a partially analogous situation now. There is an undeveloped mountain West awaiting the touch of genius and industry and there are doubtless thousands of service men who would be glad to turn to this most desirable development very much as service men did in the after period of the Civil War. There are, of course, differences in condition, and the mountain lands are not so ready to answer man's call as were the prairies; but with a helpful policy on the part of government these lands can be made available for limitless contributions to the sustenance of the Republic and the compensation of those who participate in developing them.

It does not matter whether one thinks that agriculture is the inspiration of great cities and their supporting industrial areas, or whether one believes that agriculture is inspired and encouraged by the necessities of the industrial centers—they are, in fact, interdependent, and the fortune of one is inseparably linked with the fortune of the other. One thing is very certain, that intensive industrial development and the concentration of population in cities can not go on unless we have an expansion of the food supply upon which they depend for sustenance.

It is fairly contended that the American expansion of agriculture has had a very considerable part to play in the development of the great industrial centers of the Old World, as well as the magic building of our own. Nottingham and Manchester, Dusseldorf and Berlin, Turin and Barcelona, are almost as much concerned with the size of the American food surplus as are our own great cities.

When all else is said, the fact still remains that all human endeavor must be assured of an ample food supply else nothing is to be accomplished. It is not to be said that we have outlived the world's capacity to produce a surplus of agricultural products, but, confessedly, we have got out of a properly-balanced proportion in the development of our agricultural supply. Much of the world, of course, remains undeveloped. It is said that the plains of Siberia, or the productive tropics, could accommodate the world's population with an abundance of food, but the trouble is that the great, virile, progressive peoples of the world are not inclined to live in Siberia, nor are they attracted to the tropics. As a matter of simple truth they lose the distinct activity and aggressiveness when taken out of the zones of present-day activity.

It is perfectly useless to talk about transplanting populations. The practical tasks of life are to make old Mother Earth contribute to the call of population wherever it may be located. Thus transportation becomes the key to the problem of supply.

The inter-mountain and Pacific West is endowed with riches known to no other region of the world. We came to a new appreciation of these riches during the anxieties of the World War. Necessity and a new realization of self-dependence led us to appraise the vast deposits of phosphates and the lakes of potash and the mines of tungsten, and we revived the production of silver and added to the output of lead and copper, because the warring world had no other such dependable supply. We turned to the abundance of spruce for our aeroplanes, and the rare metals for alloys, and we found the limitless abundance of coal and used it to bunker the shipping of the Pacific. We increased the supply of the long staple cotton, and of wool, and of meats and fruits. Whatever it was that the world greatly needed and was listed in our own necessities, we discovered a goodly and reassuring share of it in the vast storehouse of the almost untouched natural resources of the great West.

During the war we made a good deal of progress toward development of these resources, because the war made rapid and intensive effort necessary. But with the end of the war there came a tendency to slacken development. We find that some things were started, and then neglected or forgotten. With correct vision of a long future, contemplating continued growth, we might well recognize that to this inter-mountain empire we must turn for the same service as that rendered by our central plains when they were brought into productivity following the Civil War.

Our vision, then, of the ultimate development of the mountain empire, reveals a great region, developed uniformly, with regard to all its variegated possibilities. I have never been able to think of "reclamation" as connoting merely the construction of ditches, and dams, and reservoirs, to put water on dry lands. In my view this has been only a phase—though a most important phase—of reclamation. I have believed that our mountain West is one day to be one of the richest and most completely self-contained economic areas in the world. My vision of the future pictures it as a wonderland whose streams are harnessed to great electrical units, from which flows the power to drive railway trains, to operate industries, to carry on the public utilities of cities, to smelt the metals, and to energize the activities of a teeming population.

Not long ago, a great journal of the South published an interview in which I attempted to suggest my hope and aspiration for the new South as a developed, renewed and finished community, based on the proper and complete utilization of all its opportunities. I have a similar thought about the possibilities of the mountain West. The "Great American Desert" disappeared out of our minds and geographies long ago, but we have retained the impression that our Rocky Mountain area could never sustain populations and industries comparable with those of the central valley, or the East, or the South. This has done injustice to the Far West. The richness of its mountains, the power of its streams, the productivity of its valleys, the variety of its climate and opportunity, the possibility of its dry areas, all suggest its destiny to become the seat of an ideal civilization.

I undertake to say that there is no region in all the world whose resources could be developed to the utmost, with greater benefit to the world as a whole, and America in particular, than our mountain West.

It requires no effort of imagination to contemplate, a few generations hence, our country as a land of from two hundred to three hundred million people, with a third of them happily planted in this area.

We have come to the time when the problem of our Far West is one of wisely directed development, rather than of too much conservation, or, perhaps, to put the thought more accurately, the bringing about of a degree and character of development which will constitute the wise form of conservation. One can not go on saving all of nature's bounty and be fair to the generations of to-day. I do not mean that the time has come to break recklessly into our treasure house and squander its contents; but I do decidedly mean that we can not longer delay encouragement and assistance to rational, natural and becoming development. We must have that far-western awakening which shall prove an effective corrective of the concentration of population and the regional specialization of industry which has been repeatedly called to our attention and has inclined to make of us a sectional America.

Conservation, it must always be kept in mind, does not consist in locking up the treasure house of our natural resources. That would be the most objectionable form of waste. Conservation, in its truest sense, consists in the judicious use of the resources which are ours. The conservation policy in its application to coal is not the same as in its application to the forest. Coal, once it is taken from the earth, can never be replaced; the forests, by proper care and attention, may be made to yield a never-ending return. The conservation policy, as applied to rivers and streams, presents still another phase, since the tree which we leave standing in the forest, and the coal we leave lying in the mine, remain for the use of those who may come later on, while the water which flows unused to the sea is lost beyond reclaim. It is impossible, by the utmost utilization of our flowing waters, to affect to the extent of a single drop, the automatic and eternal replenishment at the source. Emphatically, therefore, in the case of our water-power resources, there is not even a seeming paradox in saying that the more we use the more do we save.

The only problem in the conservation of waters is to see to it religiously that this great inheritance of the people is not monopolized for private enrichment, and of this there can be little danger if the state—and the nation, when it has the jurisdiction—shall wisely exercise the powers of regulation which it possesses in respect to all public utilities.

In a somewhat different manner, the same principle will apply to our other natural resources. Emphasis must be placed upon their use rather than upon their storage, only it must be a use which, while providing for the present needs, must keep an ever watchful guard upon their preservation for the need of generations yet to come.

Theodore Roosevelt had a clear vision of the vast possibilities of our West. In a chapter of his autobiography devoted to "Natural Resources of the Nation," he says: "The first work I took up when I became president was the work of reclamation." In his view, reclamation, conservation and proper utilization, were all parts of the same program. That must be our view to-day. "It is better for the government to help a poor man to make a living for his family, than to help a rich man to make more profit for his company," declared President Roosevelt. This he laid down as one of the principles upon which he based his policy toward public land areas. The principle is particularly sound to-day. We have need to make these areas the seat of millions of new American families, just as we broke up our prairies and distributed them among strong, enterprising, vigorous men who developed them into the great states of the Mississippi Valley.

We must make our mountain West a country of homes for people who need homes. It has everything that they will need. It can provide them with food, with the materials for industry, with lumber from its forests, with metals and minerals from its mines, with power from its streams, and waters for the irrigation of its land. And the work must be so done that it will inure most to the advantage of society and the development of the independent, self-sustaining family unit in our citizenship. There must be proper cooperation and direction in this development, but there must be all care to prevent monopolization of resources and opportunities.

It has been intimated by some who take, I feel, the narrow view, that the industry of the East, and the agriculture of the Middle West and South, will not view favorably the proposal to develop new industry and new agriculture in the mountain country to compete with them. I confess to very little sympathy with this attitude. The sons of New York and New England built the great states of the Ohio Valley; and the sons of the Ohio Valley reared the splendid commonwealths beyond the Mississippi. The sons of every generation, in our country, have been the pioneers of some new land.

Well do I remember the covered-wagon days of the early seventies, when the resolute sons of Ohio took up the westward journey. They had little more of valued possession than unalterable determination to start afresh and be participants in the development of the wonderful land awaiting their coming. They wrought their full part in the miracle of development and gave an added glow to the westward march of the star of empire. Many who went were those who had found new soul of citizenship in the preservation of union and nationality; and it is not impossible that thousands of those who battled to maintain American rights in the world will be eager to participate in the development of the wonderland we are considering to-day. We owe to them the fullest and widest opportunities, and we owe it to them to give of government encouragement and aid in bringing about the development so much to be desired. For them and for America inestimable possibilities are in store.

To-day we are informed on the basis of statistics that if the demands of a rapidly-increasing population are to be met, new farms must be opened at the rate of one hundred thousand annually. The sad fact is that only half that number are being added to our equipment for production every year. The United States has changed, from a basically agricultural to an agricultural and industrial nation. The 1920 statistics, we are told, show that our population is preponderantly urban. More food-stuffs must be had; farms now operating will not supply present demands. The one solution is to bring more land into production.

Reclamation, as I have viewed it, means a good deal more than merely putting water on arid land. There are regions in which it means draining the water away from swamps. There are other regions in which it means restoring forests that have been thoughtlessly destroyed. There are still others in which it means frank recognition of the fact that forests have gone forever, that stumps must be removed and the land utilized for agriculture.

Nobody wants isolated communities of agricultural producers in remote reclaimed valleys, to produce things for which there is no available market. There have been some instances of this sort. But with better transportation, with encouragement to wide and varied development, the problem of markets will solve itself rapidly enough.

In dealing with our public lands hereafter we are not to be too profligate in the disposal of their resources. There has been profligacy practised in the past, though I take it that some of it was entirely justifiable, but there must be no further doling out of natural resources to favored groups. We have passed the stage when there must be exceptional bidding for pioneer development. It was against profligacy that Roosevelt raised his voice and exercised the veto power. He started the great reclamation movement and it came none too soon. Doubtless he had in mind the time when these resources must be opened for free, full and independent development. Undoubtedly, if he were alive to-day, he would be a cordial sympathizer with the same policy of development combined with a rational policy of conservation of resources for Americans yet to come, all of which is consonant with square dealing with all Americans engaged in the fulfillment of our obligations of to-day.

It is all a forward-looking program with an ever mindfulness of the passing day. The great change in our whole economic situation, and the realization that our opportunities of providing for increased population have a definite limit, must enforce this view. Roosevelt performed a great service to the nation, and what he did for his time we must carry forward to the future. I would not have the West return to the era of speculative operations, tending to monopolies. I want to see, as he did, a development of our public land country which will insure the utmost equality of privilege and opportunity.

In some places private capital, in others public funds can best do the work that is required. I have no particular preference for either program, except that I would like to see in each instance the policy that will on the whole best serve the national purpose. I would not hesitate to employ federal credit for certain types of reclamation work, and on the other side I would not stand in the way of having that work done by private enterprise, if this seemed best.

Western states desirous of cooperating with the federal government in reclamation contemplate enactment of uniform laws to aid in financing reclamation work in conjunction with the federal plan of impounding waters. Lack of unified effort and policy has been a misfortune in the past, and the time has come for a fixed and comprehensive program.

In broadest contemplation, we must keep in mind the thing which inspires all of our activities. I have an abiding conviction that American nationality has been the inspiration from the beginning. We found that inspiration renewed and magnified when we made sure of indissoluble union and started afresh for the supreme American fulfillment. The impelling thought now is to go on as Americans, free and independent and self-reliant, to make the United States a great Republic, unafraid and confident of its future and rejoicing in American accomplishment.

XI

SOCIAL JUSTICE
A Message for Women

When we all acknowledge that the time and the conditions of the world call for fuller recognition of human rights, the protection of the life of human beings and the conservation of our human resources, it becomes the duty of the women of America, and it becomes my duty, to deal with these matters of social justice upon a high plane of an idealism which is not too proud to work. More, it is our duty to consider without hypocrisy or high-sounding phrases a program of action. And it is my duty to address not only you who are women, now entering by justice, by the principles of sound democracy, and by the wisdom of a progressive civilization, into citizenship, but also to address every American who is interested in our common welfare.

I pledge myself to support with all that is in me whatever practical policy of social justice can be brought forward by the combined wisdom of all Americans. Nothing can concern America, and nothing can concern me as an American, more deeply than the health, the happiness and the enlightenment of every fellow-American.

I believe that none of us can be safe and happy or reach our finest growth until we have done our utmost to see that all

Americans are safe. I believe that, if a wise God notes a sparrow's fall, no life can be so obscure and humble that it shall become of no consequence to America.

Only by reason of the depth and permanence of such belief can be founded our grave duty and our solemn obligation to consider the subject of social justice without mere emotion, without mere inspirational words, without mere entrancing phrases, without mere slogans, but with that wisdom which is needed when the desire of our hearts and heads must be translated into terms of living action and actual achievement.

The social justice that I conceive is not paternalism. It would be easy to make it so, and dangerous indeed to the best spirit that Americans can have—the spirit of expressing by the individual free will one's own merits, capacity and worth. We do not want government to suppress that expression of free will, even by benevolence, but we do mean to preserve in America an equal opportunity and a preparedness for self-expression therein, even though we use the government to do it.

Social justice, on the other hand, is not a mere sentiment. To my mind a social justice policy in government can not and should not be confined to a program for the flow of benefits from some uncertain and magic source at the seat of government. I could not even consider a policy of social justice which is conceived, as so many visionaries conceive it, as a right of mankind. I will only consider it as an obligation of mankind.

I refuse to subscribe to the doctrine which has gone so far to delude the world that even citizenship is based upon rights. I believe, and have repeatedly said, that citizenship is based upon obligation.

I will not even approach the consideration of a policy of social justice unless it is founded on the stalwart American doctrine of the duties of every one of us to all of us. The first measure of social justice to which America must always devote herself is the duty of citizenship to vote with conscience, to preserve laws, and to demand their enforcement. It is the obligation of all true Americans to live clean lives and to engage with head and hand in honest, useful production and toil.

The best social welfare worker in the world is the man or woman who lives righteously and does the task well which he or she is most capable of doing, thereby adding to the sum total of human accomplishment.

The task before us—to build high standards of social justice in America—is sometimes badly defined, and I think we all regret that the methods to be pursued have been allowed to fly without definite understanding of their landing places. Social justice, like the phrase, "self-determination of free people," is a slogan which sounds so well that the world is beguiled away from deciding what wise things may be really done about it.

For my part, I have no taste and no conscience which will allow me to talk to Americans with phrases which I myself can not define and with a program which is not practical and capable of fulfillment.

Let us be practical in our idealism. Let us plan the things we can wisely do, and then do them.

I believe that there is no step more practical, no step which will mean more to the growth of America's social welfare; no step which will guarantee better America's social justice, than one which I now propose to you.

There can be no more efficient way of advancing a humanitarian program than by adapting the machinery of our federal government to the purposes we desire to attain. While others may have their eyes fixed on some particular piece of legislation, or some particular policy of social justice which calls for the sympathetic interest of us all, I say, without hesitation, that our primary consideration must be the machinery of administration, and when the time comes for us to recognize our admin-

istrative government in Washington, we must all stand together for the creation of a department of public welfare.

It is almost useless for us to go on expending our energies in
advancing humanitarian policies which we wish put into effect,
and it is useless for us to hope for the effective administration
of humanitarian policies already undertaken by the federal government, until we have prepared to create an administrative center for the application of our program.

At the present time we find social welfare bureaus and social
welfare undertakings scattered hopelessly through the departments, sometimes the one overlapping the work of the other,
and sometimes, indeed, engaging in bickerings between themselves. The picture is one of inefficiency and of wasted funds.

Let us not only have social justice and social welfare developed to the fullest extent which a wise citizenship will approve,
but let us have also the means with which to make social justice
and social welfare real and functioning, rather than visionary
and inefficient.

I have no doubt that there will be some who will find in this
proposal cause for calling me an extremist, but when we have a
task to do, which has been dictated by our conscience and ap-
proved by our wisdom, let us straightway find the way to do it.
I do not say this without a word of caution. I recognize certain
dangers which are always presented when government under-
takes large and detailed tasks. I have said already that we must
avoid paternalism, and that we must avoid it because a paternalistic social welfare program would smother some of the liberties, some of the dignity, and some of the freedom for self-
expression of our individuals.

In creating federal departments for the administration of social justice and social welfare, we must avoid the fearful results
of bureaucracy. I am inclined to think that as between a bureaucracy of a military power which paid little attention to the

regulating of domestic affairs, and a bureaucracy of social rules and regulations, the latter would oppress the soul of a country more. We do not want, and we will not have, either in America. Undoubtedly the great blessings of our Constitution, appearing, indeed, as if our Constitution had been written by the hand of Providence, are the checks which it places upon the development in a national center of a great bureaucratic paternalism. We are momentarily irritated at times when we desire to enact measures, which appear to be dedicated wholly to the welfare of mankind, when we find that constitutional limitations prevent their legality. But we have been saved through these many years; and will be saved throughout America's continued progress from the growth of too much centralism, too much paternalism, too much bureaucracy, and too much infringement of the individual's right to construct his own life within our American standards of reason and justice.

I would like to point out to all America that there is grave danger at hand when centralized expression begins to take from local communities all the burdens of social conscience. The best that humanity knows comes up from the individual man and woman through the sacred institutions of the family and the home, and, perhaps, finds its most effective application in the community where life is personal, and where there is not an attempt to cut men and women to a given pattern and treat mankind as a wholesale commodity.

I like to think of an America whose spirit flows up from the bottom and is not handed down from the top. I like to think that the virtue of the family is the combined virtue of its members, and that the virtue of a community is the combined standards of virtues of its citizens. I like to think of a nation whose virtue is the combined virtue of its communities. For such is America; such may she always be!

So long as her expression flows up from the people, and not

down from a centralized autocracy, however that autocracy may label itself, America will live in all her virile strength. When we create in Washington a strong federal government and undertake, even for the most humanitarian purposes, new federal burdens, let us with all reverence pray that we shall never by this means put to sleep the spirit, the sense of duty, and the activities of the communities and neighborhoods of the United States. I raise these cautions, not because I am doubtful of the wisdom of the federal government doing all that it can to conserve the human resources of the United States, but, on the contrary, because I believe we must move forward upon a sure footing, without undertaking impractical or unwise programs which lead to disillusionment, and in the end retard, rather than accelerate, the expression of American conscience and its application to the welfare of the people.

With these cautions, however, guiding us as we go forward to create, if possible, the right kind of federal machinery for social justice, we will feel more confidence in creating a federal department of public welfare. When making the proposal for a department of public welfare to America, I am aware that I have made a step in advance of any platform. I have chosen to speak to you on the practical question—the question of how to do the tasks we must do, the things American conscience is calling to have done.

We all know that we face tasks of social justice, which we must undertake with despatch and efficiency. Who can suggest one of these tasks which can supersede in our hearts, or in the rank which foresight and wisdom will give, that of the protection of our maternity?

The protection of the motherhood of America can not be accomplished until the state and the nation have enacted and, by their example, have enforced customs, which protect womanhood itself. I know full well that there are women who insist that women shall be treated upon the same basis that men are treated. They would have a right to take this position in their own behalf, but I insist, and all true Americans must insist, that no woman speaks for herself alone. She is the possessor of our future, and though she becomes engaged in the task and services of civilization, we must preserve to her the right of wholesome maternity.

We no longer are speaking of a small group. Twelve million women in the United States, forty per cent of them between fifteen and twenty years of age, are engaged in paid occupations or professions. Such an army of potential maternity demands from America careful and adequate protection in the conditions which surround their labors. For such an army there must be an increasing enlightenment in industry and business which will tend to break down distinctions of sex in matters of remuneration, and establish equal pay for equal work. The needs of such an army, engaging in the tasks of America, probably can not be understood by men alone. In the administration of federal and state laws, and in the educational services which will assist industry and the public, and the women themselves, to understand the needs of women, we will require the services of the most capable women we can get upon federal and state boards of employment, labor adjustment and, indeed, wherever the welfare of maternity and the welfare of American childhood, directly or remotely, are involved.

There is a growing and a probably wise sentiment in America in favor of an eight-hour day everywhere for women. The federal government has set the example in a policy which looks toward the protection of our best human resources. Justice and American standards demand that women who are employed should be paid a living wage, and it is entirely unfair to the state which fulfills its obligations to humanity in any piece of humanitarian legislation affecting industry, if other states, by failing to perform their obligation, gain a temporary advantage in costs of production. I believe that one of the principal functions of the department of public welfare will be to enlighten and educate local action, so that we may have throughout our states an increasing sense of obligation to meet a national standard of social justice.

I desire particularly to emphasize the need of safeguarding the prosperity of the American farmer, so that he may compete with industry in obtaining labor. I am hearing constantly voices raised in behalf of the women in industry. I desire to raise mine now in behalf of the women on the farms of the United States, who in the labor shortage of this year have gone into the fields—young girls and old women—to give a service which, if it had not been given, would have deprived us this year of an adequate food supply. There must be labor, normal labor, available to farm as well as factory.

One of the important organizations under a department of public welfare might well be the children's bureau which now exists, but whose work, already proved so useful, must be extended and made still more capable of educating and assisting in pre-natal care and early infancy. It is for us a grim jest, indeed, that the federal government is spending twice as much money for the suppression of hog cholera as it spends for its entire program for the welfare of the American child.

We are not doing, however, enough for the future citizens of America if we allow women to injure, by industry or ignorance, their maternity, or if we allow infancy itself to go unprotected from disease and unintelligence. Among sixteen important countries of the world, thirteen show a lower death rate for mothers than the United States, and six show a lower death rate for very young children. Nearly a quarter of a million babies—practically a number equal to the entire casualty list of our men in the great war—die every year.

It will not be the America we love which will neglect the
American mother and the American child. The program to prevent abuses of child labor, already greatly advanced, represents
the progress of legislation toward wise prevention, which will
receive the sanction of constitutional law. When we first legis-
lated to remedy the abuses of child labor, approximately one out
of five children between the ages of ten and fifteen in the United States was a wage-earner. I do not say that among them there
were not many exceptions, whose labors were of such a nature
as to fit them to become better men and women, but I do say
that in the mass, their labor represented the theft of their right
to childhood, to happiness, to health, and of their right to prepare to embrace our equal opportunity, to realize for America
their capacity and worth as future citizens. This condition we
could not neglect, and we can not neglect the problems of child
labor in this country. Even if it were not upon humanitarian
grounds, I point out to you that the protection of American maternity and childhood represents economic thrift. Indeed, it represents the saving of our blood, our posterity, and the future
strength of our nation.

Next to maternity and childhood, I believe that our attention
must be centered upon our national health. Between twenty-five
and thirty-three and one-third per cent of the young men examined in our first draft for war were found to be defective, or
physically unfit. Examinations of children in the public schools
of America disclose that fifty per cent of them are suffering from
physical delinquencies, most of which proper attention would
remedy before maturity. I believe, therefore, that we must undertake with great seriousness the problem of our national
health. I am alert to the danger of too much oppressive bureaucracy in any great federal health bureau, but I want to see the
various agencies grouped together in a department of public
welfare. I want to see their principal function, that of stimulat-

ing, by research and education, the communities and local governments of the United States to the most active and sufficient campaign against low standards of physical well-being. We must attack, first, a low standard of health among children; secondly, the invasion of diseases which attend a low standard of morals; and thirdly, the invasion of epidemics, and the neglect of the chronic diseases of maturity, many of which are due to a failure on the part of individuals to adjust their living and habits to an artificial civilization.

It is not possible to discuss in detail all of the measures of social justice which sooner or later the people of this country will probably have to consider and adopt and put into action, or reject as impracticable. But I do conceive an obligation of government, to devote grave attention to another group of problems which are all humanitarian, and which are of vital importance to our future.

I have spoken of my attitude toward industrial peace. I have stated my full belief in labor unionism and in the practise of collective bargaining, and I have also tried to emphasize a belief, which I feel deeply, that industrial peace, though it may be attained by adjustment and conciliation, can never stand upon its firmest foundation until a higher sense of loyalty to the task permeates the workers, and a higher sense of humanitarian brotherhood permeates the employers of America. I do not think of this reawakening of a higher conscience upon both sides in terms of generalities, and I regard it as being one of the humane functions of which our government is capable to saturate the industrial life of our country with a spirit which will tend to reunite parties of discord.

We are often presented with conditions which result in industrial controversy, but which may not be charged to either side. I speak specifically of two examples: The first involves the unrest, the discontent, which arises from unsteady employment.

It is not a condition to be remedied alone by federal employment bureaus filling in the gaps of unemployment, but rests largely upon conditions of industry which make for seasonal production and periodic closing and opening of industrial plants and occupations. I am enough of an optimist to believe that government can assist in the abolition of this most unfortunate condition. I am even enough of an optimist to believe that the government can take a large part in a second and, perhaps, even more important campaign. I believe that many of our workers are engaged in tasks which have been so specialized that the men and women themselves have become almost pieces of mechanism. This has produced a condition in which many of our workers find no self-expression. In such a condition, men and women are drained dry of the impulse to create.

Without any false notions as to the possibilities of turning back progress so that the day of less specialization may return, I none the less believe that it is our duty as a whole people to see if we can not make every job in the country a small business of its own. No matter how simple the job, be sure that it plays a dignified and an essential part in our welfare. The man who does it must learn to realize it; and more than that, he and his employer must combine to make every job, no matter what it is, a friend of the man who does it—a friend because the man who does the work has learned an interest in it, so that just as if it were his particular individual business he may understand how he may improve that job, so that he may understand its unit costs, its bookkeeping, its purposes, its relation to other jobs, and to the whole fabric of our national production, and so that the job may become, as much as possible, day by day, an expression of human being.

This is our program of social justice. I have not attempted to make it complete; who can do so? This is my program for a department which as an effective government agency will further social justice. I have not attempted to describe it in detail. No one can describe it in detail before it becomes a working organization; but I believe that I have voiced the conscience and the common sense of America when I say that we must pay new attention to the conservation of our human resources.

I must not fail to speak of one of the measures of social justice and social welfare not often catalogued in this manner, but perhaps more important than any we have considered. I refer to the enforcement of law. It will not be my business to decide what laws shall be. It will be legitimate for me to invoke public opinion for their enactment, but such a call to public opinion must be based more upon the duty of the executive of the nation to give facts to the people than upon his desire to give opinion, theory and propaganda. The enforcement of the law is an executive responsibility and must be undertaken by the executive without regard for his personal approval or disapproval of the law, which it has been the people's will to enact. Whatever your achievement may be in the world, your concern, as mine, is principally with the American home and you, with me, will realize that we must have throughout the land a respect for law-abiding principles. We must all condemn without qualification the failure of enforcement of prohibition, just as we must all condemn the failure of established authority to prevent outrages of violence, such as lynching.

I appeal to you as to enforcement of law because I regard the enforcement of law as a fundamental principle of the American conscience, and if I am to distinguish between men and women, I will attribute to the women of America the major part in the preservation of that conscience.

THE VALUE OF PLAY
A Message for Youth

From time immemorial the nations and races which have been fit to assume leadership in the world were those whose people knew how to excel in athletic sports and had not forgotten how to play—and how to play hard. The great civilizations—those which have left a profound effect upon the development of mankind, those which have contributed not only to exploration, to the extension of orderly government, to supremacy of arms but even in greater measure to the thought and philosophy of the world have been the nations that developed athletic sports—who have known how to play. There was Greece, famous for the original Olympic games; there was Rome, that for centuries kept alive the customs of athletic competition in her arenas; there is the United Kingdom, great extender of enlightenment to far corners of the earth. Japan, leader in the Orient, built her power and her alertness by a tradition of training in competitive games such as wrestling and sword play. And, thank God, there is America, the stronghold of liberty and the square deal, which still can take the honors in the world's competitions in healthy sports.

I believe that play, not mere entertainment, not reading comic strips or "passing the time," as some say, but real play, play that gives a man or woman a chance to express himself or herself as an individual, is one of the finest assets in our national life and one of the best builders of character.

I believe there are reasons behind the fact that the nations that have led the world have fostered athletic games and know how to play, how to express their spirit through play, how to develop character through competition and how to let off turbulence of the spirit and wasting restlessness and discontent of mind and poisons of the body through good hard play.

Nothing is more important to America than citizenship; there is more assurance of our future in the individual character of our citizens than in any proposal I, and all the wise advisers I can gather, can ever put into effect in Washington.

We may as well go back to that sound idea right now. America will never rise higher than the merit and worth of her combined individual citizens. No nation ever has, none ever will.

I regard play as having no small part in the building of citizenship. I do not mean play for children, I mean play for everybody. The war left us nervous and irritable. As time goes on we are going to see that an industrial age will inevitably concentrate men in cities. The business executive, unless he looks out, will die at his desk—not his body perhaps but his spirit, and the worker, particularly the man behind the machine who makes only a few motions over and over again each day, will have no means of self-expression and his spirit will die too.

There are other reliefs that we must provide for these evils that threaten us, but the renewal and the preservation of a national custom of play and of athletic sports is vital to preserve the fitness of our citizenship.

Competition in play teaches the square deal. Competition in play teaches the love of the free spirit to excel by one's own merit. A nation that has not forgotten how to play, a nation that fosters athletics is a nation that is always holding up the high ideal of equal opportunity for all. Go back through history and find the nations that did not play and had no outdoor sports and you will find the nations of oppressed peoples.

I am making no appeal that I will not be willing to have tested by the standards that good competitive sport has set up in all ages and among all fair men. These are the standards of a good citizenship which is willing to play the game. I want behind me only those who are willing to play the game. We have had too much encouragement from Washington given to the man who wanted to cut second base, or get something for nothing. In the first place, that is not a square deal to the rest of us; in the second place, there is no way to make a delivery that is worth anything.

I have not said anything yet about the effect that wholesome play has upon national health. We received a rude shock when during the war we came to examine physically that part of our population that is commonly called "the flower of American manhood." We examined in the first draft a little over two and a half million men and not counting those who were rejected later at mobilization camps, the percentage of rejections on account of physical unfitness went right along day after day between twenty-five and thirty-three and a third per cent.

Do you know what that means? It means that one out of every three or four young Americans in their prime—between twenty-one and thirty—is unfit. And although I am not a doctor, nor even a professor, I will take a chance and say that most of that unfitness came from unwise eating, sleeping, bad habits and no play, no exercise, no working out the poisons in good sweat, no adjustment of the human frame by stretching it in competitive effort.

Nevertheless in spite of the need for play to bring back American bodies to health, so that health may be the sacred heritage of children yet unborn, I put, even above the boons of health that play gives, the greater treasures that it confers and always will confer upon nations that preserve its customs and its morals—the treasures of honor and a sense of fair play.

XII

FRATERNITY
A Message for Knights and Ladies

The world has found itself lately very much committed to the idea of fraternity. It is the natural outcome of a new understanding of our relationships. Fraternity is one of the most natural things in life. You have seen it in the organization of men into small groups, of women in their societies. You often see it in the animal world, where nature has somehow implanted love of life and at the same time the love of fraternity and association together, and if you stop to think about it you will discover that in animal life there is the fraternity of protection and mutual advancement. This finds expression in our human relationships in various forms. I do not suppose there is a people in all the world that has so developed the fraternity idea as we have in the United States. I have sometimes wondered how many fraternal orders there are, secret and open.

But we find fraternity in all the walks of life. It is a curious stage in human affairs when we have run really to excess in some forms of organization. It is only a development of the tendencies of men and women of common aspirations to get together to further their very natural interests. In a broader sense we have come a little nearer to a fraternity of nations.

The World War brought us to a new realization, that mankind, after all, is interested in one common purpose, namely, the uplift of mankind. Nations that were once looking at each other in envy and jealousy and rivalry have come to understand that their best interests are to be served in mutual advancement, and we have come to the stage in human affairs where we are seeking to put an end to warfare and to conflict and to dwell in a little closer understanding.

I know full well the impelling thoughts in any helpful organization. You seek to advance the standards of individual life; you seek to advance the standards of your common activities. You would not go into an organization if you did not think that, individually and collectively, you would be better off because of the association which you undertake. And at the same time, while that is your impelling thought I know that not a single one of you would go into any fraternity that was ever proposed if you thought it involved the surrender of anything you hold essential to your own individual life.

I recall many an obligation that I have come in contact with in secret orders, and there isn't one that ever asked a man to surrender any of his liberties, any of his freedom of thought, any of his freedom of religious belief. And making the application of that point I want to apply it to nations. Just now we are talking very much about associations of the nations of the world. We, of America, gave first the finest illustration that was ever recorded of a fraternity of nations. I like to recall it. I have spoken of it on previous occasions. Some twenty years ago, when America had first planted the flag of this Republic, with every glittering star fixed, as a banner of hope and stability in the Orient, there broke out in China what was known as the Boxer Rebellion. The rebellious Boxers in their warfare endangered all the foreign residents in the city of Peking. It became necessary to send a military expedition to the relief of those beleaguered citizens of the various nations of the earth. And I always like to recall that a son of my own State of Ohio led the military expedition, the late General Chaffee. They brought about the relief of the citizens of foreign countries imprisoned in Peking, and in a little while the military forces were withdrawn. Then representatives of the several nations engaged in that expedition sat about a table and figured out the expense of the several countries that had sent military relief. The sum presumably necessary to pay the United States for the protection of its citizens was assessed against China, and a like sum, or proportionate sum, was assessed against the government of China for Germany, for Great Britain, for France, and the other nations involved.

Later on we came to cast up the accounts in detail, and we found that the government of China had paid eight million dollars in money to the United States more than was necessary to recompense us for our military endeavors. And the United States returned that money to China, sent back eight million dollars that they had paid us in that award—the first time that such a thing was ever done in the history of the world. That was the first great illustration of a fraternal spirit among nations. And that is why China plants its faith in the example, in the democracy, in the justice of the United States of America. And we are greater to-day by reason of the example which we then set to the world than we could ever hope to be by force of arms, no matter how large our army and navy may be.

An interesting aftermath resulted in the Peace Conference in Paris. China went into the war at our request. I do not know that you recall it but that Oriental people, at the suggestion of the State Department of our country, declared war against the Central Empire, Germany and Austro-Hungary. And when the war settlements came about China sought to be represented at the Peace Conference and they ought to have been represented. For some reason or other they were not. Then they said, "We will trust the United States of America to represent us, with confidence in that great Republic." And yet, somehow in the Peace Conference, through contract secretly made, China had no voice in the settlement and instead of being awarded the freedom of her own people under the gospel of self-determination for which America spoke, several million of her people were delivered over to a rival nation, with the consent and approval of those who spoke for America in Paris. But when that covenant came into the United States Senate, I rejoice that there were Americans in the United States who said "No" and that we did not approve of the Shantung award. And we kept the plighted faith in the lesson we taught China some twenty years ago.

Now, the obligation and the fraternal thought, as I said a little while ago, is that you would not enter into any fraternal organization, no matter how high its ideals might be, if you thought it involved the surrender of anything essential to your individual existence. And that is precisely the doctrine I am trying to preach just now for the United States. We want to be high and eminent and influential in the fraternity of nations. We want to play our part in the promotion and maintenance of peace throughout the world; aye, we want this Republic to play its part in assuring justice to all the world and in advancing human kind in every way we can. In America we want to contribute our part through the application of justice rather than the application of force; and if I can have my way of speaking for America we will never enter into a fraternity that is founded on force. But we do mean to play our part, our full part, along the lines of justice properly applied.

So with this new international relationship proposition, we are saying that we do not intend to go in so long as it involves the surrender of anything essential to the dignity, freedom of action, freedom of conscience of the United States of America.

But we do willingly say that we want to join any association of nations for the promotion of justice, for the felicitation of international conscience; aye, for turning the deliberate, intelligent public opinion of the world upon international controversy so that it may be settled in the applied conscience of nations rather than through military force directed by a council of foreign powers, with capacity to invite, aye, to order the sons of America into war for the protection of the boundaries of nations across the sea. That America will never consent to. We have our own destiny to work out, and we in America have been working it out to the astonishment and the admiration, yes, to the inspiration, of all the world.

I have an abiding conviction that America can play her greatest part in the furtherance of mankind by first making sure of the character of our citizenship at home, and then give to the world the American example rather than the word of a Republic assuming to meddle in the affairs of the nations of the earth.

I am infinitely concerned about promoting the spirit of fraternity at home. We of America have made a great Republic. We have developed material America, and we found out in the World War that we needed spiritual America. I never can forget a development during the early days prior to our entrance into the war, when the Senate was discussing the enactment of the armed ship bill. That is, the bill which was to provide for arming our merchant ships for their protection against submarine warfare. A citizen of Marion—and I knew him well— wrote me and said: "Senator, why are you so anxious about protecting American rights? Don't you know, sir, there is no such thing as a distinctly American citizen?" This from an American. When I answered him, I said: "Maybe it is true, as you have written me, that there is no such thing as a distinctly American citizen, but if that startling statement be true, then, in God's name, out of this turmoil of the world, out of this travail of civilization, let us have a real American come from Columbia's loins to leave us a race of Americans hereafter."

So the World War brought us to a realization that we had developed material America, we had prospered, we had advanced in education, in art, in world influence and had attained a high place in world eminence, and yet although we are a blend of the peoples of the Old World, we had given very little consideration to the development of American spirit. And I am preaching the gospel from this time on of the development of an American soul; from this time on I am preaching the gospel of the maintenance of American spirit, of the development from this time on of a fraternity and a loyalty that will make us all, no matter whence we came, American in every heartbeat.

You can not go on in any other way. Here in America we have no racial entity. We are a blend or a mixture or an association of all the nations of the earth, but, unhappily, up to the time of the war we were very much a collocation of peoples; but from this time on we want to be a fraternity of Americans. From this time on we want to continue to emphasize the necessity for the elevation of the standard of American citizenship, not in spirit alone, but an elevation of the conditions under which men and women live.

XIV

THE VILLAGE

A Message for Happy Americans

I have been thinking of the wonderful development of the Northwest. We take things so readily for granted that we never stop to think what made us what we are. In the brief time we have been building this wonderful country of ours, we have been working to the perfection of a new civilization and a habitation and a condition which are the pride of all Americans. And it is a very wonderful thing to contemplate how much we have accomplished in less than a century; and when you stop to think about it, it is all worked out with patience and continued endeavor in the right direction. Nothing great is brought about by the wave of one's hand. You can not have miracles in the development of a country, and yet in this wonderful land of ours, with the Constitution only a hundred and thirty-three years old and our Western civilization less than a century, we have outstripped every other civilization in the world. That is a tribute to American accomplishment. And when I look back upon it, I find myself asking—Why must we be so impatient with the continual working out of the processes of human advancement? It takes time and understanding and an abiding faith to do this. So I want you all to have faith in this country of ours.

I am reminded of the thought, which has oftentimes been in my mind, that there is no audience to which I more delight to talk than that which can be assembled in a village community. I grew up in a village of six hundred, and I know something of the democracy, of the simplicity, of the confidence in—aye, better yet, of the reverence for government, and the fidelity to law and its enforcement, as it exists in the small community. I do not believe that anywhere in the world there is so perfect a democracy as in the village. You know in the village we know everybody else's business. I grew up in such a community, and I have often referred to it as a fine illustration of the opportunities of American life.

There is no social strata or society requirement in the village. About everybody starts equal. And in the village where I was born the blacksmith's son and the cobbler's son and the minister's son and the storekeeper's son all had just the same chance in the opportunities of this America of ours. I wonder if it would interest you if I told you about what happened to some of the boys with whom I went to school? I like to refer to it because it is the finest proof in the world of the equality of American opportunity to the sons of this Republic. In the class when I was a boy there was Ralph. Well, Ralph was a bruiser among the boys and I would have picked him out for a prizefighter. Man grown, I looked him up. I had not seen him for thirty years, and instead of finding him a pugilistically inclined citizen, I found him at the head of the bank in the village where we grew up, as peaceful and able as any man in the community. Then there was Wheeler. If there was any boy in our crowd who started with greater advantage in money, he was the fellow. He had inherited three thousand dollars—and that was an awful amount of money in those days. But Wheeler went the wrong way, and came to failure. Then there was Frank. Frank was the village carpenter's son; but Frank to-day is one of the great captains of industry in Chicago, and before the World War advanced salaries and compensation, he was getting twenty-five thousand dollars a year. A Village Boy! Then there was Ed, the cobbler's son. He wanted to be a geologist. He had once heard a geologist lecture. So he started to study geology, and in order to study to more advantage, because his father was not able to send him to college, he became a Pullman car conductor, to study as he worked. What do you think became of Ed, aspiring to become a geologist? Ed turned out to be a preacher and he is a great preacher this day. And so I might run on—but I must tell you about another one. Let us say that his name was Charlie. He was the local grocer's son. Well, you would not have thought he had any special advantage but his father loved him and sent him to college. He is one of the great lawyers of Ohio to-day and he measures his wealth in large figures and he never cheated anybody out of a cent. Then there was, let us say, Henry. Henry was the brightest boy of his class. The teacher always pointed him out as the pride of the school. He was the one to whom we always had to look as an example of youthful brilliancy in the village. We were all envious of him. What do you suppose became of this brightest luminary of them all? I found him in a village, the janitor of his lodge, and in spite of his less important achievements he was the happiest one of the lot. What is the greatest thing in life, my countrymen? Happiness. And there is more happiness in the American village than any other place on the face of the earth.

So I like to preach the gospel of understanding in America, the utter abolition of class and every thought of it; the maintenance of American institutions, the things we have inherited, and above all continued freedom for the United States, without dictation or direction from anybody else in all the world.

XV

TWO WARS
A Message for Veterans

When I stop to think of the long period that has passed since our G. A. R. Veterans went to the front in 1861 it brings to me a new realization of what they did, first in service to country in preserving nationality and second in laying down arms and returning to citizenship, giving to the country the leaven of patriotism.

From my earliest recollections I have a distinct remembrance of Civil War soldiers in their activities of citizenship and their marked influence in political progress. If the millions of sons who went forth in the defense of our national rights in the World War can turn to a new birth of patriotism as you did, that will compensate us for all our part in the great world struggle. The man who goes forth to offer all on the altars of country returns a better patriot. We need a new birth of patriotism in our country.

Our veterans didn't enter the war to free the slave, although that was a becoming ideal. They didn't go to war because they hated any group in the South or to establish any new conception of justice. But they entered the conflict because they found the Union was threatened; they went to save the Union and nationality.

There have been a variety of opinions as to why their grandsons went to war. Their sons went to war with Spain for humanity. Some have said that their grandsons went to war for democracy and some that they went forth to insure that there would be no wars in the future. If we went to war for democracy, shouldn't we have gone in when it first started? And if we went to war to insure that there would be no more wars, shouldn't we have gone in before so many millions had been sacrificed?

The simple truth is that their grandsons went to war when Congress made the declaration because our nationality and rights had been threatened. Then it was possible to call the sons of America to battle.

That doesn't mean that when the war is over we should surrender what we went in to maintain. If it is within my power, there will never be a surrender of that which you have handed down to the generation of to-day.

THE MEANING OF THE ARMISTICE
A Message for Patriots

November the eleventh has an abiding significance to America and the world. For America it sealed our capacity to defend our national rights and stamped our effectiveness in aiding to preserve the established order of world civilization; for the world it marked a new order for humanity, and for all time it warns ambition and madness for power that one man's or one people's domination of the world never was designed by God and never will be tolerated by mankind.

The day is especially interesting to our own country, because without American participation it might have been a later and a different date, if indeed there had been an armistice day at all. We do not claim to have won the war, but we helped mightily and recorded undying glory to American arms and gave the world a new understanding of the American spirit and a new measure of American resources.

Whatever the world may have thought of us before, however incorrectly we may have been appraised, the world has come to know that selfishness is not a trait of our national character, that commercialism does not engross us, that neutrality was conceived in fairness—not in fear—and that when our national rights are threatened and our nationals are sacrificed, America is resolved to defend, and ever will. More, we gave to humanity an example of unselfishness which it only half appraised before misunderstandings led to confusion.

We helped to win the war, unaided and unmortgaged. We fought with the Allied Powers, and were never committed, if fully aware of them, to the compacts of the alliance.

History will record it correctly, no matter how much beautiful sentiment has beclouded our purposes in the World War. We did not fight to make the world safe for democracy, though we were its best exemplars. Nor did we fight for humanity's sake, no matter how such a cause impelled. Democracy was threatened and humanity was dying long before American indignation called for the Republic's defense. But we fought for the one supreme cause which inspires men to offer all for country and the flag, and we fought as becomes a free America, and dropped hatred and stifled greed when the victory for defense was won.

We proved anew that there is a free and ample America, which does not ask, but freely gives. We were American in name before the World War made us American in fact, not a collection of peoples, but one people with one purpose, one confidence, one pride, one aspiration and one flag.

We learned a lesson, too, of transcending importance. Righteousness and unfailing justice are not in themselves a guaranty of national security. We must be ever strong in peace, foremost in industry, eminent in agriculture, ample in transportation. Better transportation on land and an adequate merchant marine would have speeded our participation and shortened the conflict. I believe an America eminent on the high seas, respected in every avenue of trade, will be safer at home and greater in influence throughout the world.

I like to think of an America whose citizens are ever seeking the greater development and enlarged resources and widened influence of the Republic, and I like to think of a government which protects its citizens wherever they go on a lawful mission, anywhere under the shining sun.

All the way from my home in Ohio to the furthermost port on the Gulf I have seen among the people who came to give us kindly greetings scores of stalwart, virile young Americans who served their country so gallantly and effectively at home and overseas. One must have cause for renewed pride in the character of these men, in their readiness and capacity to serve, in the certitude of their manhood, in their new baptism of Americanism. These soldiers of the Republic, like their fathers, believe in an America of civil and human and religious liberty, they believe in an America of American ideals. They believe in America first, for it is in America that their hopes and inspirations center.

We choose no aloofness, we shirk no obligation, we forsake no friends, but we build in nationality, and we do not mean to surrender it.

Our young veterans believe it is only morning to the life of the Republic and they want to look forward to the surpassing noonday of national life, where this Republic shall be the foremost nationality among the nations of the earth. I believe with them and with you that our sure path is the American path. I do not believe the wisdom of Washington and Jefferson and Hamilton is to be ignored, nor are the chivalry of Lee and the magnanimity of Grant to be forgotten, nor can the supreme belief of Lincoln in union and nationality be forgotten nor the outstanding Americanism of Theodore Roosevelt fail to stir our hearts.

THE FEDERAL CONSTITUTION
A Message and a Memorial

America uncovers in observance of the 133rd anniversary of the birthday of the nation. I do not say the birthday of American freedom, which we celebrate variously, though always patriotically, on July 4, in reverence for the Declaration of Independence, but this day is the anniversary of the literal birthday of our American nation.

I can never forget that, in the beginning, independence was one thing and nationality quite another. The Declaration of Independence was the proclamation of the representatives of the colonies, animated by a common purpose and aroused by a common oppression. They were brought into a comradeship of suffering, privation and war, and the magnificent Declaration of Independence was the bold, clear statement of human rights by an association of fearless men who knew they were speaking for liberty. It might have been the declaration of any people anywhere who had equal reasons and like aspirations, because it is the most comprehensive bill of rights in all the annals of civilized government. Under the Declaration, the colonies fought for freedom, and then in the chaos of victory they turned to nationality as the necessary means of its preservation. In short, freedom inspired and nationality was invoked in order to preserve.

We take it all so much as a matter of course now, that we little appreciate the marvel of the beginning. One may well wonder that the colonists succeeded in their warfare for independence, because they were battling against the commanding power of the Old World. They were little prepared, they were lacking in resources and they knew nothing of concord, except in the universal desire for freedom. It is well to remember that the colonies were not imbued with any thought of a common purpose except for freedom itself. There was no distinctly American spirit which was common to them all. They were strung along the shores of the Atlantic Ocean and widely separated by miles of distance and by leagues of primeval forests and they were much more separated by the diversity of the origin of their population, by differences in religion, in ideals and manners of life. The whole thought of their association was that of an offensive and defensive alliance against foreign aggression, and there was no suggestion of a national feeling or aspiration before, during or immediately following the successful War for Independence.

Indeed, there were conflicting interests of sections and states, there were wide diversities of opinion, especially with respect to the merits of royalism and democracy, there were envies and jealousies, there were differences of methods and varieties of practises—all making a situation in which it was difficult to commit the free colonies to anything more than the futile articles of confederation.

Almost a decade passed before the dream of erecting upon this new continent a great and strong nation "dedicated to liberty" became a compelling vision, and forced its way upon the waking, active hours of the more progressive and thoughtful men of the colonies. It is even true that a fundamental federal law was not in contemplation by most of the delegates who assembled in the first convention, and many of those who attended would not have been present had they known that such a work was to be undertaken. Surely a supreme federal government was not in the minds of a majority of the delegates. In that convention were men of every type of mind. There were Puritan and Cavalier, Quaker and atheist, autocrat and peasant, Yankee and slave-holder. Among them there were, even as there are now, the extremists who favored autocracy or the commune. Under other names, but easily identified with present-day prototypes, they had the reactionary, Bolshevik, Socialist, Republican, Democrat, Prohibitionist, Liberal and what-not.

It was difficult timber out of which to erect the enduring temple of the Republic, and I think it worth our while to recall this to lead us to greater appreciation. I can well believe that the hand of destiny must have directed them; and the supreme accomplishment was wrought because God Himself had a purpose to serve in the making of the new Republic.

The formulated work of the convention of 1787 was not contribution, even in fundamentals, of one mind. The best men in the colonies were among the delegates, and it is inspiring to recall that the president of the convention was George Washington. It is equally pleasing to note that this great man, born to wealth and position, allied by blood to the titled aristocracy of England, said to be the richest American of his time, commander-in-chief of a victorious army which idolized him, who had put resolutely away the offer of a crown offered by men who could have delivered it, stood steadfastly in this convention, as always, for a republican form of government.

The debates of the constitutional convention show that every known form of government had its advocates; that every proposition presented was discussed, amended, revised and reviewed, again and again. The result was in every instance, compromise or conviction, as must be the case when the collective judgment and not the individual will is sought.

There were many times when it seemed that the convention must adjourn in impotence. The strain upon mental and physical and nervous energies was exhausting. Public feeling ran high and fear of a war between the colonies was justifiable. It was the venerable Franklin, sage and patriot, who at a critical time, asked the convention to cease from its labors, lay aside its differences, and reverently and trustfully invoke the Divine guidance. And I am one who firmly believes that that prayer was answered.

Out of this chaos of opinion, out of this rivalry and conflict, out of this ferment of New World liberty, came the great experiment, the first written constitution evolved in the history of the world. It was not the product of any one mind. I have always thought Hamilton to have been the inspiring genius, though Madison contributed very largely, and Franklin's wisdom was never ignored. Probably no conclusion could ever have been reached without the compelling efforts of Washington. It was not the matching of minds except in the spirited debate. Such a document was of necessity the result of a meeting of minds in unselfish, conscientious and truly patriotic purposes. I believe such a meeting of minds in high purpose to be the most effective agency possible in the conduct of public affairs.

It has been said by those who disparage our government that our Constitution contains nothing new fundamentally. That might be said of the Sermon on the Mount; it might be said, and truthfully, of the components of any plan, or theory or practise in government, or science or religion. But in combination, in essence and results it was new.

William Pitt said of the American Constitution: "It will be the wonder and admiration of all future generations and the model of all future constitutions."

Gladstone said: "It is the greatest piece of work ever struck off at a given time by the brain and purpose of man."

James Bryce, the most distinguished and unprejudiced commentator upon the Constitution, said: "History shows few instruments which in so few words lay down equally momentous rules on a vast range of matters of the highest importance and complexity." And for illustration, he observes that our Federal Constitution with its amendments may be read aloud in twenty-three minutes; that it is only about half as long as Paul's first epistle to the Corinthians—and only one-fortieth part as long as the Irish land act of 1881.

It was Pitt who spoke with the spirit of prophecy, for our Constitution in essentials has been the model for every constitution formulated by civilized peoples since its enactment, and every government but our own has materially changed in form since ours was established by the adoption of the Constitution of 1787.

And what did this Constitution do? It provided a practical, workable, popular, central government upon the representative plan, while reserving to the people in the states and their political subdivisions the control of their local affairs. It provided a government of checks and balances, which made the will of the majority determinable and effective, but protected the rights of the minority.

It was written in six months to meet an impending crisis, and it was written to provide a central government for the people of thirteen scattered colonies, having a total population smaller than now lives within the confines of several of our cities, and yet it was so soundly conceived and so masterfully written that its provisions fully meet the actual governmental needs of a hundred and twenty millions of people, as well as the conditions which are revealed in an experience of a hundred and thirty-three years—and, I believe, of all the years to come.

It provides for a free government of free men. Under it there is freedom of thought and expression, freedom of worship, freedom of action within the law and the rights of others.

Under it there is no reason for revolt, no necessity for resort to violence. Any cause which can enlist a majority of the free, untrammelled electors of this land may, under the Constitution, win its dominance. The will of the people, expressed at the ballot boxes of the Republic, can change our government, as well as its policies, may even abolish the Constitution itself.

This fact should make us even less tolerant of the lawless men who seek to establish, by threat or violence, the rule of minorities or of classes, which inevitably becomes autocracy or anarchy.

The patriots of 1787 devised a government to do the things so wonderfully and graphically expressed in the preamble:

"We, the people of the United States, in order to form a more perfect union, establish justice, insure domestic tranquillity, provide for the common defense, promote the general welfare, and secure the blessings of liberty to ourselves and our posterity, do ordain and establish this Constitution of the United States of America."

Can any of you, my friends, conceive a clearer statement of a noble purpose? Can you suggest the insertion or elision of a word or phrase which would improve it; can any one name a single ideal of popular government which is not covered by its beautifully concise, but comprehensive, phraseology?

And the constitutional provisions are as clearly stated and as patriotically conceived. Let us look for a moment into the fundamentals of our Constitution.

It provides for three departments of government: the legislative, the executive and the judicial—the legislative to make the laws, the executive to administer and enforce them, the judicial to interpret and construe them.

The legislative power was vested in Congress, and the provisions relating to Congress are wonderful in the far-seeing wisdom of the constitution-writers. It was provided that Congress was to be composed of a Senate and a House of Representatives. The latter to be the popular body; its members to be elected by the people every two years. They were to be chosen from districts erected upon the basis of total population. This was intended to give equality of representation throughout the country. These districts, under the proposed apportionment, were to be small enough so as to have only one or few dominant interests; this would bring all interests under consideration in the house. The members were to be elected for two years—thus giving the electors frequent opportunity of selecting their representatives and sending them with fresh mandates from the people.

The Senate was intended to be the deliberative body—the check and brake upon the wheels of legislation. Its members were to be elected from the state by the legislatures thereof and for a term of six years. This was to give stability to their positions and remove them from the influence of temporary excitement. As the members of the house came from districts based on population giving the larger states or communities a preponderance of power and strength in that body, the rights of the minority—and the smaller states—were safeguarded by a provision that every state should be entitled to two members of the Senate. Could anything be fairer or more practical than these provisions? Under them we had in the most practical form the so-called modern idea of the initiative, referendum and recall. Any district through its representative could initiate a bill; the right of petition to Congress was established. That gave the initiative. The election of a new Congress every two years gave an opportunity for the referendum and recall.

And it worked. No proposed legislative matter having the

support of any considerable minority of electors ever failed of introduction or consideration by Congress.

The "Founding Fathers" were determined to maintain the independence of action of the three departments of government. They provided that the president should be elected by persons appointed as electors by the states, but they provided also that no member of Congress or officer of the government should be an elector.

They provided that the president should have the veto over the acts of Congress—but they provided that Congress, by a two-thirds vote, could nullify his veto.

In the constitutional convention it was proposed that the judiciary should be appointed by the Senate—but it was held that this would place the judges under obligations to the Senate. Then it was proposed that they should be appointed by the president, and it was held that this would make the judges subservient to the executive and give him power to override the courts and set aside the will of the people as expressed in law. And so the convention provided that the judges should be appointed by the president with the advice and consent of the Senate.

At first the power to make treaties with other governments was proposed to be conferred upon the Senate, but it was agreed finally that there should be a division of responsibility and power. And despite the construction placed upon the language of this provision, I ask your attention to its statement: "He (the president) shall have power, by and with the advice and consent of the Senate, to make treaties, provided two-thirds of the Senators present concur." Can any American wonder that members of the Senate, in complying with their solemn oath of office, insisted upon safeguarding America when the president proposed to submerge our nationality in a super-government of the world?

Looking back now, it is easy to understand that the fathers of the Republic had no reasonable conception of the mighty possibilities in its development, nor did they begin to appreciate the magnitude of the great thing they accomplished in writing the fundamental law, and yet somehow a sense of the tremendous importance must have been upon them. Bancroft wrote: "The members were awestruck at the result of their councils. The Constitution was a nobler work than they had believed it possible to devise."

Our nation is one and one-third centuries old, which is but a very brief period in the story of mankind. There are some rare instances in which three generations in one family stretch from the immortal beginning to the wonderful now. I have, myself, in these later years, met great-grandchildren of those who participated in the making of the Constitution, yet in that stretch of time we have grown to be the greatest Republic on the face of the earth, and the work which the fathers did in their day still lives in full force as the fundamental law of the oldest living Republic.

This makes it easy to understand why the constitution-makers did not appreciate the greatness of their achievement. They stood too close for full realization, but we may contemplate it to-day in the revealing light of history and from the view-point of American accomplishments. One by one European autocracies have yielded, until, in the last great onrush of democracy, practically all nations have been engulfed, even steadfast and solid Britain has shaken off the control which her aristocracy wielded for centuries, and has raised her House of Commons to practically unrestricted authority.

America alone among the great nations of the world has undergone no change or vicissitude which in itself has not proved to be strengthening, both materially and spiritually. An anchor our Constitution has been called, but if it be so regarded it can not be held a rigid, immovable thing, but rather as a sheet anchor, serving only to keep the great ship safe and steady on her course; because there is nothing inelastic in our basic law. Almost immediately the "Bill of Rights" for men was added and now, by the votes of men, the yet more striking "Bill of Rights" for women has been adopted.

During all these years the Constitution has never failed America and despite heedless assertions to the contrary which occasionally reach our ears, America has never failed the world. Not only has she afforded a safe refuge and unrestricted opportunity to oppressed beings everywhere, but by showing that "liberty with law is fire on the hearth, but liberty without law is fire on the floor," she has proved democracy itself. Far more by force of example than by force of arms, she has shattered the idols of monarchy and brought thrones crashing to the ground. And now, as ever before when distracted peoples are in the throes of a rebirth of nations, she stands ready, and let us hope, will be in a position, through earnest cooperation of all branches of our government, to lend a helping hand. To "America First," as pledged by the individual, I would add simply as addressed to the nation, "To thine own self be true."

Under the Constitution we have prospered and developed; under the Constitution we have kept alive the watch-fires of freedom and have maintained the open door of liberty. Under the Constitution we have seen millions of people, self-governed, self-controlled, work out their destiny in ordered liberty. Under the Constitution we have worshiped God in accordance with conscience without hindrance, and we have seen the reins of power transferred from hand to hand, in bloodless revolution, at the peoples' behest.

Under the Constitution we have welcomed the oppressed or unfortunate of every land, and shared with those who desired and deserved our heritage and citizenship.

Under our Constitution, with the amendments so readily made when major settlement is evoked, every man and every woman may have an equal voice and vote in the government which he helps establish, maintain and direct. Under it the rights of each and all are guaranteed. Every citizen is made, so far as our imperfect human nature permits, safe in his person, his property, his rights of every kind.

No honest man, who loves his kind, can ask more than that. When he does not receive that, the fault is all or partly his own, and flows not from failure of plan of government, but from failure of performance.

We date our independence to the memorable July day in 1776 when the bell of Independence Hall "rang out liberty" to all the peoples of the world. I know that the confederation of colonies was the great, the essential step toward the consolidation of victories of the Revolution, but it was the ratification of the inspired Constitution of 1787 that first established us as a nation. I want it to abide; I want it to impel us onward; I want the Republic for which it was conceived; and I want the Republic governed in America, under the Constitution.

XVIII

THE NATIONAL CONSCIENCE
A Message for All Americans

The conservation of human resource is even more important than the conservation of material resource; but I desire to call your attention to the fact that one depends a great deal on the other, and that the two form a benevolent circle. This fact is forgotten by many persons. On the one hand, there are those with a strong sentiment to improve the conditions of the less fortunate or by a policy, even more wise, to prevent the development of unjust social conditions or low standards of health and education, and to maintain our position as a land of equal opportunity. So fixed do some of their eyes become on the human resources of America and on occasional misery and suffering, that they even become impatient with those who are working to build up, by industry, wholesome business enterprise and productivity, the material resources, and, consequently, the standards of living of our people.

On the other hand, there are other persons who, in the main, I believe, are not heartless or selfish but who are so intent on their tasks of manufacturing and commerce, driven perhaps by that impulse for creation which is so often misinterpreted as mere money-hunger, that they forget that the men, women and children about them, sometimes in their employ, are not mere commodities and are not even mere machines to be consumed, worn out, treated without love and tossed aside, but are human beings whose welfare in the end is so intertwined with that of every other human being that the imperfections, the poor health, the neglected old age, the abused childhood, the failure of motherhood in any one of them becomes an injury and a menace to us all.

We must bring together the broadened consciences of those who concentrate their attention upon our business and our great enterprises on the one hand and see only the vision of prosperity, and on the other, those who find in their hearts and minds no vision but that of raising the standard of health and happiness of less fortunate human beings, where such standards have fallen below those which all Americans wish to see enjoyed by all Americans.

Service to America,—that must be the spirit of all our citizenship—Service, a willingness to serve intelligently, to train for humane service, to cleave to an idealism of deeds and honest toil and scientific accomplishments, rather than to serve by mere words.

I believe this spirit can be fostered best by uniting America. I believe it is best served by wiping away distinctions of class, creed, race or occupation which separate Americans from Americans.

I say, let us awake the conscience and intelligence of the social reformer, and even of the discontents, and the agitators who, sometimes, with fine zeal for the good of mankind, nevertheless go too far and do gross harm to mankind by spreading the idea that productivity, a day's honest work, American business, and commerce are somehow the symbols of evil, of oppression, of selfishness. These are not symbols of evil, nor are business and industry, expressing the toil of head and hand, the enemies of man's welfare. They are the sources of man's welfare.

We must awaken the conscience of the ignorant and the misguided to the fact that the best social welfare worker in the world is the man or woman who does an honest day's work. We must awaken their conscience to recognize that American business is not a monster, but an expression of God-given impulse to create, and the savior and the guardian of our happiness, of our homes and of equal opportunity for all in America. Whatever we do for honest, humane American business, we do in the name of social welfare.

But it is equally true that we must awaken the conscience of American business to new interest in the welfare of American human beings. It is not enough for America that her business and commerce shall be honest; they must also be humane. Men, women, and children of America are not commodities. To treat them as commodities is not only to forget the responsibility we owe to the brotherhood of man, but also it is to be blind to the fact that American business can not flourish nor the material prosperity of America be built upon a firm foundation until by just such work as by protection of health, by education, by the preservation of wholesome American motherhood and vigorous and happy American childhood, and a national humane spirit finding expression in enactment of law when need be—we insure the welfare of our human resources.

The belief which I would like to send to all Americans is my belief that we can not have the fulness of America until all of us turn again to love of toil and love of production, to respect for honest organization of effort and to a willingness to put all our shoulders to the wheel. But with it goes my belief that we can not have all that love, and all that respect, and all that willingness until throughout the organization of our industry and commerce there runs the flow of love of man.

The End

Index

Actors: must know characters, 64

"Advice and consent": and appointment of judges, 127

Aeroplanes, 83

Africa, 75

Agriculture, 35, 39; and colleges, 41; end of exploitation, 44; need for voice in government, 47; interdependence with industry, 82, 118; in Middle West, 87; in South, 87

Algebra, 70

Alliance: compacts of, 118

Allied Powers, 118

"All the world's a stage," 65

Ambition, 26

Amendments: and guarantee of constitutional rights, 130

"America First," 18, 34, 73, 74, 76, 77, 129; believed in by soldiers of the republic, 119

American business: not big business, 15; the daily work of the nation, 16; suffered from government meddling, 18; and the welfare of human beings, 133; not a monster, 133; as God-given impulse to create, 133

American farmers: consideration in trade relations with other countries, 52; and availability of labor, 97

American ideals, 47; justice not force, 109

American products: best in the world, 26

American resources, 117

American Revolution, 121

Americans: must know soul to play part in world civilization, 65; one in three unfit, 104. See also Foreign-born Americans

American spirit: development of, 111, 117

American stage: desire for it to be best, 65

Anarchy, 124

Arbitration, 28

Argentina, 51

Arithmetic, 70

Armed Ship Bill: discussed in Senate, 110

Articles of Confederation, 121, 130
Armistice Day, 117
Artistic merit: of silent drama, 65
Association of nations: for world peace, 13, 107; desire to join, 110
Atheism, 122
Austria-Hungary, 108
Automobiles, 33

"Back to the land" movement, 41
Balkan states, 76
Ballot boxes, 124
Bancroft, George (1800–1899): quoted on importance of Constitution, 128
Baseball, 31, 104
Bill of Rights, 120; for women, 129
Boundaries: protection of foreign, 110
Boxer Rebellion, 107–9
Bryce, James (1838–1922), 124
Budget Bureau, 19
Business, 15, 17, 20–21, 103, 131–32

Cabinet: proposed new office for education, 72
Capital: harmonized with labor and management, 24–33
Captains of industry, 113
Casualty list of Great War and death rate of babies, 97
Censorship, 65
Central government: provided for by constitution, 124
Centralism, 94
Chaffee, Gen. Adna R (1842–1914), 108

Character: developed through competition, 103; of citizenship an example to world, 110
Children, 97–99; as future citizens, 78; protection of, 79; welfare of, 96; money spent for welfare of, 97
China, 107–9
Citizenship, duties of: preserve laws and demand enforcement, 92; vote with conscience, 92
Civil liberties, 119
Civil War, 39, 81, 83, 115
Class consciousness, 31–32, 73–75, 114, 143
Closed shop, 32
Coal, 71, 80, 83, 85
Collective bargaining, 32
Colonists, 12, 120–21
Congress, 41, 54, 116; power under Constitution, 126
Conscience: above party (political), 78
Conservation, 59–60, 81, 85, 88, 121
Constitution, 53, 74; and bureaucratic paternalism, 94, 112, 123; has lasted, 124; meets needs of people, 124; Land Act, 124; what it is and does summarized, 124; James Bryce on, 124; length of, and conditions, 124; provides for freedom, 124; fundamentals reviewed, 125–27; as anchor, 128; established nation, 130; benefits of, 130
Constitutional Convention of 1787: delegates not of one mind, 122
Cooperative associations: and

buying, distribution, and selling of farm products, 37; right of farmers to form, 48

Copper: in mountain West, 80, 83

Corinthians, Paul's epistle to the: length compared to Constitution, 124

Corn belt, 47; half of land farmed by tenant farmers, 50–51

Cost of living, 30, 71

Cotton, 83

Country school, 70

Covered wagon days (1870s), 87

Cummins-Esch Bill: restores railway ownership, 29

Death rate for children in United States: compared to casualty list of Great War, 97

Debates: of Constitutional Convention, 122

Declaration of Independence, 120

"Do unto others as you would be done by," 14

Draft: men physically delinquent, 78, 98, 104

Education, 25, 57; department of, 69; recognized in law, 71; federal control of, 72

Eight-hour day, 96

Electors: under Constitution, 124; appointed by states, 127

Electricity: and lengthened reading period, 58

Employers, 24; humanitarian brotherhood, 99

Enforcement of law: as executive responsibility, 101; as measure of social justice, 101

Engineering: scientific pursuit of, 61

Epidemics, 99

Equal opportunity, 32, 96, 104; in development of public land, 89

Europe: diplomats and honesty, 61, 73

Excess profits tax, 17

Executive orders and laws: failing to serve business, 17

Executive responsibility: promoting business, 20

Exports, 40

Extension departments (agricultural), 41

Fair play, 105

Faith, 112

Farmers: addressed as patriotic citizens, 34; role of in World War, 72; as individualists, 46; organization of, 37

Farm loans: principle of, 36; Farm Loan Act, 50

Farm organizations, 46–47

Farm prices: during the war, 43; stabilization of, 48; need better understanding of factors that influence, 49

Farming: as commercial, scientific operation, 41; as independent and self-respecting activity, 44; contemplated in broadest possible way, 53

Far West: destiny of, 84

Federal boards of employment: need for women on, 96

Federal Bureau of Education: influence of, 69

Federal government: supreme,

122; influence on recognition of teachers, 70, 95

Federal Health Bureau: part of department of public welfare, 98; functions of, 98

Fiume, 72

Food surplus, 82

Forbes-Robertson, Sir Johnston (1853–1937), 66

Foreign-born Americans, 34, 77; as means for reaching all Americans, 73; addressed as Americans, 73; love for kinsfolk, 74; appeal to Senate on behalf of land where kinsfolk reside, 75; danger of conflict among, 75; ill will not wanted, 76; need to know, 79

Founding Fathers: and independence of departments of government, 127

France, 108

Franklin, Benjamin: philosophy recalled, 61; and Constitution, 123; invoked divine guidance, 123

Fraternity: wholesome human traits, 75; as organization of men, 106; to further natural interests, 106, 109; reason to join, 107; spirit of promoted, 110; of Americans, 111

Free colonies: and Articles of Confederation, 121

Freedom: of religious belief, 62; of speech, 62

Geology, 114

Germany, 82, 102

Gladstone, William (1809–1898): on the Constitution, 124

Government: departments summarized, 125

Grand Army of the Republic, 115

Grant, U. S., 119

Great American Desert, 84

Great Britain, 82, 102, 108, 128

Great-grandchildren, of writers of Constitution, 128

Greece, 102

Hamilton, Alexander, 61, 119, 123

Harding, Warren G.: and God's guidance, 14; consistency of statements of, 22; promotes good fortune, 23; and "life without toil," 24; and railway ownership, 29; on self-sustaining nation, 45; on paternalism and incompetency, 47; on produce and conserve, 47; favors Farm Loan Act, 50; on buy from America, 52, 93; on landhogs who menace our future, 52; and department of public welfare, 54; on maternity and childhood as guarantee of security of U.S., 56; on woman suffrage, 56; on honest people, 60; and clear vision, 61; rejoicing to be American, 68; as good teacher, 70; and citizens' pride, 75; warning of to foreign born, 77; and groups of foreign background, 77; and foreign capital, 77; vision of for intermountain West, 83; and new South, 84; nationality inspires, 89; on private capital, 89; on development of West, 89; on social justice, 90; on citizenship obligation, 91; and practical idealism, 92; and paternalistic welfare program, 93; and American spirit, 94; on maternity and childhood protection, 98; and unsteady employment, 100; on small business, 100; on failure to enforce laws, 101; and fraternity, 109; and international relationship, 109; on village opportunities, 113; and surrender of gains, 116; on selfishness, 117; on hatred and greed, 118; and World War making us American, 118; and government as protector, 119; on Declaration of Independence, 120; on meeting of minds, 123; on Constitution, 124; on Senate and supergovernment, 127; on productivity, 132; on toil, 132–33; on industry, on commerce and love of man, 133

Health: standards of, 78, 131–32

Henry V (Shakespeare), 67

Hog cholera: suppression of, 97

Home: cost of, 28; teachers should know, 70, 133

Homestead Law, 39, 41

Honesty, 35; old standards, 60; needed to prevent industrial and social unrest, 61

Honor, 105

House of Commons (Great Britain), 128

House of Representatives, U.S., 126

Hyphenated Americans, 34, 73–74, 76. *See also* Foreign-born Americans

Ideals: differences among colonists, 121

Independence Hall, 130

Industry, 25–26, 28, 78, 82, 84, 87, 99, 118

Initiative, 126

Interior, Department of, 72

Irish Land Act of 1881: length compared to Constitution, 124

Italy, 76, 82, 102

Jackson, Andrew, 61

Japan, 102

Jefferson, Thomas: belief in equal rights, 61; wisdom of, 119

Journal of the South: interview, 84

Judiciary, 127

Julius Caesar (William Shakespeare), 65

Labor, 24, 33; "life is labor, or labor is life," 22

Land speculation, 38

Law: to protect American workers, 133

Lee, Robert E., 119

Liberty, 119–20

"Liberty with law is fire on the hearth, but liberty without law is fire on the floor," 129

Lincoln, Abraham: sympathy and steadfastness recalled, 61; belief in Union, 119

Linotype machines, 58

Livestock and grain production balance, 43

Lynching, 101

Machinery of federal government, 92

McKinley, William, 61

Madison, James, 123

Mail carriers, rural, 58

"Make the world safe for democracy," 118

Management: harmonized with capital and labor, 33

Manners: differences of in colonists, 121

Mansfield, Richard (1854–1907), 67

Manufacturing, 131

Markets, agricultural, 88

Meeting of minds: Constitution as result of, 123

Melting pot, 73

Merchant Marine, 18; arming of, 110, 118

Military force: directed by foreign powers, 110

Minority rights: safeguarded by Senate, 126

Mississippi River, 38, 81, 87

Monopolies, 89

Moral degeneracy of war: cunning, ruthlessness, and greed, 60

Mothers: role of society in training and guidance of children, 54–55, 95, 132; and teachers, 55

Moving pictures, 63–65

National health: need for protection of, 78; importance of, 98; and play, 104

Nationality: threatened, 116; not to be surrendered, 119

Natural resources: present needs of future generations, 86

Navy, U.S., 108

Newspapers, 27, 57–59

Oath of office: senators and, 127

Old age, 132

Old World: standards of raised, 30; strife from meddling, 75, 111; commanding powers of, 121

Olympic games, 102

One America, 77

Oppressed peoples, 104; welcomed, 129

Outrages of violence: failure to prevent condemned, 101

Parenthood: responsibility of shifted to teachers, 69

Paris Peace Conference (1919), 108

Passing of the Third Floor Back (drama), 67

Paternalism, 91, 93–94

Patriotism, 115, 124

Pioneers, 87

Pitt, William (1759–1806): on the Constitution, 123–24

Poland, 76

Politics, 23, 58, 65

Postal service, 19

Practical idealism, 92

Prayer, 123

Press: must remain free, 62; can render service, 62

Price-fixing: of farm products, 49

Private capital vs. public funds, 89

Profiteering, 31, 36, 50

Prohibition: enforcement of, 101, 122

Protective policy: prosper America first, 30

Public land: profligacy practiced, 88–89

Public utilities, 84

Public welfare: proposed department of, 93, 95, 97–98

Pulpwood: Canadian prices for, 59; forest consumption imperils supply, 59; imports from Canada, 59; New England supply exhausted in twenty years, 59; New York State supply exhausted in ten years, 59

Quakers, 122

Race, 76, 111, 132

Railroads, 29, 51, 61, 84; workers, 30

Railway legislation. *See* Cummins-Esch Bill

Reading, 70

Recall, 126

Reclamation: and idle land, 44, 83; and Roosevelt, 86, 88; defined, 88

Referendum, 126

Religion, 13, 55, 1192, 121

Roosevelt, Theodore: Americanism of, 119; awakening recalled, 61; and conservation, 88; denounced profligacy, 88; great service of to nation, 89; and principles of public land use, 86; on reclamation, 86; and vision of possibilities of west, 86

Rural free delivery, 57

Russia, 34, 61, 76, 82

Ruth, Babe (1895–1948), 31

Schools, 50, 55, 64, 69–73, 103–4

"Self-determination of free people," 92

Selfishness, 117

Senate, U.S.: advice and consent, 75; and Armed Ship Bill (1917), 110; as deliberative body, 126; rejected Shantung award, 109; role of in treaties, 127

Sermon on the Mount, Matthew 5–7, 123

Service, 77, 132

"Shoulders to wheel," 133

Slacker on the job: cheats fellow workers, 24

Slavery, 115, 122

Socialism, 29, 122

Social justice: actual achievement, 91; not paternalism, 91; based on obligation, 91; visionaries reject, 91

Social reformer, 132

Social welfare: inefficiency of bureaus of, 93; workers defined, 133

Society: and children, 54

"Something for nothing," 104

Soviet Union. *See* Russia

Spanish-American War, 116

"Sparrow's fall," 91

Spiritual America: need for shown by World War, 110

"Square deal," 102

Submarine warfare, 110

Supergovernment of world: submerge nationality of America, 127

Switzerland, 80

Tariff, 17, 51

Teachers, 69, 70, 72

Telephone, 58

Theater, 62–64, 66

Thrift, 26

Toil, 132
"To thine own self be true," 129
Transportation, 82, 118
Treaties: and Senate, 127; president's power, 127

Unionism, 32
United States: as self-sustaining nation, 45; expenditures for theater, 63, 77; population two to three hundred million, a third in the West, 84; change to agricultural and industrial nation, 87; fraternity idea developed, 106; returns money to China, 108–9
U.S. Army, 108, 117

Veto, 88, 127
Violence, 124
Visionaries, social justice conceived as a right, 91
Vote, 92

Wages: high for efficiency, 23
War for Independence. *See* American Revolution

Washington, George: wisdom of, 61, 119; warned against alliances and meddling abroad, 76; president of Constitutional Convention, 122; for republican form of government, 122; and Constitution, 123
Women: citizenship of, 90; working age, 15–20, 96; and suffrage, 54, 56; need for protection in war, 96; equality, 96; remuneration, 96; needed for federal and state boards, 96; essential to food supply, 97
Work: love of, 26
Workers, loyalty to task, 99; as pieces of mechanism, loss of creativity, 100; laws to protect, 133
World War, 42–43, 73, 83; effects of, 103, 107, 110; and material America, 111, 114, 115; reasons for American entry, 116; purposes in fighting, 118

Youth: inspiring to teach, 69